D1557655

# Lyndon Johnson Remembered

# Lyndon Johnson Remembered

*An Intimate
Portrait of a Presidency*

Edited by Thomas W. Cowger and
Sherwin J. Markman

**ROWMAN & LITTLEFIELD PUBLISHERS, INC.**
Lanham • Boulder • New York • Oxford

ROWMAN & LITTLEFIELD PUBLISHERS, INC.

Published in the United States of America
by Rowman & Littlefield Publishers, Inc.
A Member of the Rowman & Littlefield Publishing Group
4501 Forbes Boulevard, Suite 200, Lanham, Maryland 20706
www.rowmanlittlefield.com

PO Box 317
Oxford
OX2 9RU, UK

British Library Cataloguing in Publication Information Available

**Library of Congress Cataloging-in-Publication Data**

Lyndon Johnson remembered : an intimate portrait of a presidency /
edited by Thomas W. Cowger and Sherwin Markman.
     p. cm.
Includes bibliographical references and index.
  ISBN 0-7425-2798-0 (hardcover : alk. paper)
  1. Johnson, Lyndon B. (Lyndon Baines), 1908–1973. 2. Johnson, Lyndon
B. (Lyndon Baines), 1908–1973—Political and social views. 3. United
States—Politics and government—1963–1969. 4. United States—Social
policy. 5. United States—Economic policy—1961–1971.
6. Presidents—United States—Biography. 7. Johnson, Lyndon B. (Lyndon
Baines), 1908–1973—Friends and associates. I. Cowger, Thomas W., 1955–
II. Markman, Sherwin, 1929–
  E846.J54 2003
  973.923—dc21

                                                                2003001963

Printed in the United States of America

For our wives (mother and daughter)
Peggy Markman and Vicki Cowger

For a century we labored to settle and to subdue a continent. For a half a century we called upon unbounded invention and untiring industry to create an order of plenty for all of our people. . . . In your time we have the opportunity to move not only toward the rich society and the powerful society, but upward to the Great Society. The Great Society is not a safe harbor, a resting place, a final objective, a finished work. It is a challenge constantly renewed, beckoning us toward a destiny where the meaning of our lives matches the marvelous products of our labor.

*Lyndon Johnson, Commencement Address, University of Michigan*
*May 22, 1964*

For the sixth and last time, I present to the Congress my assessment of the State of the Union. . . . Every president lives, not only with what is, but what could be. . . . Although the struggle for progressive change is continuous, there are times when a watershed is reached, when there is if not really a break with the past, at least fulfillment of many of its oldest hopes, and a stepping forth into a new environment, to seek new goals. I think the past five years have been such a time. . . . Now, my friends in Congress, I want to conclude with a few very personal words to you. . . . Most all of my life as a public official has been spent in this building. For thirty-eight years . . . I have known these halls, and I have known most of the men pretty well who walked them. I know the questions that you face. I know the conflicts that you endure. I know the ideals that you seek to serve. . . . Now, it is time to leave. I hope it may be said, a hundred years from now, that by working together we helped make our country more just, more just for all its people, as well as to ensure and guarantee the blessings of liberty for all our prosperity. That is all I hope. But I believe that at least it will be said that we tried.

*Lyndon Johnson, Final Address to the Congress on the State of the Union*
*January 14, 1969*

# Contents

|  | Preface | xi |
|---|---|---|
|  | Foreword<br>*Luci Baines Johnson* | xv |
| Section One | Johnson in Literature and History | 1 |
|  | They Will Never Remember Me: Johnson<br>in Historical Literature<br>*Thomas W. Cowger* | 3 |
| Section Two | Tall Texan in a Stetson: Johnson's Personality | 19 |
|  | An Uncommon, Common Man: LBJ's Pilot<br>Remembers Him<br>*James Cross* | 21 |
|  | Lyndon Johnson: An Awesome Engine of a Man<br>*Jack Valenti* | 33 |
|  | Some Aspects of Lyndon Johnson's Personality<br>*Sherwin J. Markman* | 43 |

Section Three   Measure Each Word: Johnson the Communicator      59

                Words Mattered: Johnson the Communicator          61
                *Jack McNulty*

Section Four    King of the Hill, the Great Coalition Builder:
                Johnson and Congress                              69

                Making Friends in Congress: LBJ and
                Congressional Relations                           71
                *Sherwin J. Markman*

Section Five    "I Envision an America Where . . .": Domestic
                Problems and the War on Poverty                   83

                Sending the Whole Country to Harvard:
                Lyndon Johnson's Education Revolution             85
                *Ervin S. Duggan*

                We Can No Longer Ignore Poverty in Our Midst:
                LBJ's Other War                                   91
                *Hyman Bookbinder*

                Through a Glass Lightly: Reminiscences of the
                Model Cities Act and LBJ's Dance with Legislation  101
                *Lawrence Levinson*

                Vietnam: Lyndon Johnson's Choice                  111
                *Peter R. Rosenblatt*

Section Six     The Best We Ever Had: Johnson and Civil Rights    123

                Toward a More Just America for All: Johnson the
                Civil Rights Warrior                              125
                *Nicholas deBelleville Katzenbach*

                The Wind at His Back: LBJ, Zephyr Wright,
                and Civil Rights                                  139
                *Lee White*

Section Seven   Retreat to the Ranch: Johnson in Retirement       149

                The Lion in Winter: LBJ in Retirement            151
                *Harry Middleton*

Section Eight    Epilogue: Is the Beautiful Woman Really Dead?
The Legacy of Lyndon Johnson and His
Great Society                                          159

The Great Society's Bum Rap                           161
*Ben Wattenberg*

The Ship Sails On                                     167
*Joseph A. Califano Jr.*

About the Contributors                                185

# Preface

In January 1971 a former special assistant to President Johnson, John Roche, wrote an article in the *New York Times Magazine* entitled "The Jigsaw Puzzle of History." Roche argued in that article of nearly thirty years ago that no "historically valid" treatment of the Johnson years would emerge for decades. The problem, in his view, was the unavailability of primary-source evidence. Thenceforth, he concluded, objective analysis of the Johnson presidency would have to include material from the Johnson library (which has happened) and more material from the participants themselves.[1]

Our goal in this anthology is to help fill this important void in the historiography of LBJ and his presidency by including more of the voices of these participants, particularly Johnson insiders and intimates. In other words, in the following pages the Johnson people themselves (as distinguished from scholars or critics) attempt to contribute objectively to the critically important and ongoing debate over the role of the presidency, the federal government in social programs, and in the legacy of the Johnson administration. Many of the contributors to this anthology are writing their observations and perceptions of those critical years for the first time. We have deliberately tried, where possible, to keep the editing of these essays at a minimum in order to allow the participants of those years to tell their story in their own words. The end result, we hope, will be a fuller portrait of Lyndon Johnson and his programs, a representation richer than one drawn by a single witness or from a single perspective and different from any previous works on the former president.

Our belief that such a project was needed crystallized in May 1999, when we attended what some referred to as the "final" reunion of the surviving participants in the Johnson presidency. That event, held at the Johnson Library in Austin, Texas, convinced us that the voices of those persons would soon be silenced by death and disability.

Our idea was to obtain a series of essays from those who knew Johnson best and whose work at the time encompassed the spectrum of his personality and programs. We wanted their personal perspectives of Lyndon Johnson the man as well as of Lyndon Johnson the president. Also, of course, we wanted their views—after all these years—of the continuing relevance of his programs.

In particular, we decided to focus on people connected with domestic policies or who in other ways had been intimately connected to the president. With the exception of Peter Rosenblatt's essay, which examines the Vietnam War's impact on domestic issues, we decided to avoid foreign policy and the Vietnam War. That will be saved for another anthology or for later historians. This anthology of essays, in part the result of the reunion at the Lyndon Johnson Library, is presented as a resource for interested readers and future scholars and historians.

Primarily, we wish to thank each contributor who unselfishly gave us the benefit of their recollections and insights. We want to thank particularly Harry Middleton, the director of the Johnson Library, to whom we first presented our ideas. His response was immediate and enthusiastic, and the value of his subsequent help has been immeasurable. We also wish to acknowledge Lady Bird Johnson, whose support and cooperation, both written and verbal, enabled us to obtain so many of the essays that form this anthology. Critical support—which includes resources, staff, and release time—from East Central University (ECU) greatly hastened the completion of the book. Particular thanks go to two individuals at ECU for working out the administrative details of crucial university assistance: Dr. Scott Barton, chair of the History Department, and Dr. Duane Anderson, vice president for academic affairs. We would also like to acknowledge the efforts of ECU student Joseph Owen, who diligently scanned the essays we received into a useable format. We would also like to thank Mary Carpenter, editor, History and Political Theory, Rowman & Littlefield Publishing, and her fine staff for all the support and encouragement on the manuscript. Finally, we would like to thank our families, who took part in every step of the project.

Thomas W. Cowger                    Sherwin J. Markman
East Central University                Palm City, Florida
Ada, Oklahoma

## Note

1. John Roche, "The Jigsaw Puzzle of History," *New York Times Magazine*, January 24, 1971, 14–15.

# Foreword
## *Luci Baines Johnson*

How did life in the Johnson White House affect me? It influenced my every moment then and since. I entered the White House as a child. I left as an adult.

Like every person old enough to remember, I know exactly where I was when President Kennedy was shot, and my memories of the days that follow are clearer than those of yesterday. I was just sixteen and a student at National Cathedral School for Girls on November 22, 1963. I was in a Spanish class when a girl rushed in shouting that President Kennedy had been shot. I was aghast, like the rest of the world. Unlike the rest of the world, I was to be affected on the most intimate and personal level. President Kennedy had been my friend and my father's boss. His assassination was also my first personal exposure to violent death. My mother and daddy were in Dallas with the president. I was terrified for the Kennedy family, for my parents, for my world.

My Spanish teacher had survived the Bataan Death March. Nothing seemed to affect her. She said that we didn't really know if there was truth to this tale of horror, but we soon would. In the meantime, there would be Spanish class.

In a matter of moments, the bells of the cathedral began to ring over and over again. Four hundred girls stood and walked single-file to the gymnasium, which also served as our chapel. I walked too. But all of a sudden I noticed that the line was parting to allow two girls to move forward. They were my closest friends, and my classmates. Without question, students were allowing them to cut the line in order to reach me. They propped me up as I walked, as stunned as if I had been shot myself.

Our headmistress announced that the president and Governor John Connally, our family's dearest friend, had been shot. She asked for our prayers. We prayed and were dismissed. No one mentioned whether Daddy was alive or dead. No one mentioned Daddy, period. I wandered onto the school courtyard in a daze. I saw a Secret Service agent whom I knew approach me. I realized he would only be there if the president had died. I tried to run, not to hear the wrenching truth. But there was no escaping.

It was the "worst of times," followed by the best of times. My time in the Johnson administration began and ended with apprehension for the future and respect for a role in a story far bigger than myself. Everyone I know who was in the White House during Daddy's administration says it was a time that has defined their lives. It certainly defined mine. In the beginning I saw life in the White House through the prism of its limitations rather than its opportunities. Thank God, before I left I was able to appreciate that living in the White House provided me with the once-in-a-lifetime privilege of being an eyewitness to history.

Prior to entering the White House, I had acquired every teenager's passport into freedom from adult observation—the driver's license. But a teenager in the White House is under twenty-four-hour-a-day adult surveillance by a law enforcement officer—the Secret Service. So all a driver's license is to a White House teen is the chance to operate a car, not control where you go.

Such chaperoning may have been the answer to every worried teen's mother's prayers, but to this teenager it was a nightmare. In the beginning, I saw the White House as a place of confinement—not opportunity. It was an imposing museum, a public fishbowl, and a prison. It is in fact all of those things for every First Family—but it is so much more. Luckily my attitude problem changed. But there was a roller-coaster to ride before it did.

Our first night in the White House was December 7, 1963 (the anniversary of Pearl Harbor). As a postwar baby, I couldn't understand why Mother was so distressed about having to move that day. After my husband served in Vietnam, I came to appreciate why a move on such a great anniversary would be so difficult for the Second World War generation. Mother and Daddy went out to dinner that night at the home of one of Daddy's chief staff members, Walter Jenkins. I was excited. After weeks of anguish and one official responsibility after another, we had moved into the White House. It looked like our new life could take on some normalcy. I was going to have my friend, Beth Jenkins, spend the night.

I went from feeling burdened to feeling fancy. I had a fireplace in my bedroom, a luxury I'd never even contemplated. Before the evening was over, "burden" sounded better than fancy. I knew nothing about fireplace flues. I had thought my girlfriend did; I thought wrong. In a matter of moments, a luxurious evening by the fire had turned into fear that I had set the White House on fire. After many hectic trips to the faucet in my unfamiliar bathroom, I put the fire out. I climbed onto my desk and opened my eight-foot window to let the smoke out, only to have a policeman glare up at me in my nightgown. I was mortified. Instead of spending the first week in the White House exploring, I spent it helping to paint the smoke damage off my walls. After that first night I quickly discovered what every First Family member learns—and that is that normalcy is an infrequent visitor to the White House.

My first taste of life in the White House was bitter. My father soon realized that I could be a liability to his campaign in 1964. He masterfully recognized that the way to cause me not to resent the campaign was to make me feel needed. From July 1964 to November 3, 1964, I campaigned in twenty-six states for my father. After every trip I was expected to report back on three people I had met and on three things that were important to them. This taught me how to get out of myself—a very useful gift for every teenager. It made me feel that I was an important contributor to the campaign rather than be jealous of how the campaign had robbed me of time with my family. It taught me about how people lived across the country and what was important to them. It taught me lifelong lessons about how to listen and how much you can learn from asking good questions.

As I learned, I began to fall in love with America. I began to realize just how blessed I was to have had this unique experience. But ignorance breeds prejudice. I was still pretty ignorant and therefore pretty prejudiced against the White House itself. A year later, in my senior year in high school, I wrote two term papers. One was on how White House occupants had affected the White House and how in turn they had been affected by living there. The other was on art in the White House. Through learning about those who had gone before, I came to appreciate the privilege of living in the White House and of being an eyewitness to history. I came to see the home as my Mother saw it—"the world's best public housing."

And what a privilege it was to be an eyewitness to history! On my seventeenth birthday, Daddy signed the 1964 Civil Rights Public Accommodations Act into law. This law opened our nation's buses, trains, airplanes, hotels, and restaurants to all and made it illegal to bar their use on the basis of color or creed. I had grown up in a family who deplored discrimination, but I had also grown up in the South. I knew that this was a time that would change not only my world but also my children's world forever. It was such a time of hope and thanksgiving.

I was on the front row in the Rotunda when my father signed the 1965 voting rights legislation into law. Forever a teacher, Daddy wanted me to know that it was only right that this legislation be signed in the Capitol. It was right because the courage of this Congress had made it possible for people of color to have access to the voting booths. It was right because the courage this Congress had ensured that future Congresses could include people regardless of their race, creed, or gender.

Public service was a family affair. I was among the first volunteers in project Head Start in the summer of 1965, where I learned the lifelong thrill that comes from voluntary service to your community. It's been a lesson that has brought thousands of hours of community service and millions of moments of gratitude into my life.

As a member of a First Family, I met kings, queens, princes, and princesses. I met prime ministers, presidents, and popes. I met farmers, union workers, men and women from all stations in life. I met the impoverished and the wealthy. I dined at state dinners and in countless schools, churches, and coliseums. I entertained orphans in the White House at Christmas, and I learned that every person has something to teach me, if I'll take the time to listen and to learn.

My father gave my high school graduation address as president of the United States. He crowned me Azalea and Apple Blossom Queen. But he made sure I received only five dollars' weekly allowance and that I had plenty of babysitting jobs.

I was married in the Shrine of the Immaculate Conception and had my wedding reception at the White House. But I chose to have my baby in

Austin, at its oldest hospital, because it offered me the environment of faith and support so many White House residents hunger for. I went to bed every night for a year, while my husband was at war, hearing protesters chant, "Hey, hey, LBJ, how many boys did you kill today?" I saw my father desperately searching for a way to resolve this conflict, as his tireless efforts were dashed over and over again.

One of the most painful memories I have from my White House days was watching Daddy hear of servicemen who had been injured or killed. Many a night I would sit with Daddy while he ate his dinner at 10 P.M. and watched the news. With each report of death and injury, Daddy looked like someone was lancing his gut and turning the screws. My husband and brother-in-law were there too. Lynda and I held our breaths with each report, knowing that Chuck or Patrick could so easily be the next victim. None of these men and women were statistics to Daddy. They were all sons and daughters, husbands and wives, mothers and fathers.

But one of the most relieving moments of those traumatic times also revolved around our servicemen. One evening my father asked me to find a church that would be open all night. I knew not to ask questions—just find the church. What I didn't know, I couldn't leak. About midnight Daddy told me to meet him at the South Portico. When we got in the car he told me to tell the Secret Service where we were going. We went to St. Dominic's Chapel in southwest Washington, where I joined my father on our knees. I didn't know what Daddy was praying for. I just know that I prayed for him. When we returned home, my father asked me to stay with him, as my mother was out of town. He climbed onto the bed and lay there sleepless. Around 3 A.M. he received a call. He answered and after several words of acknowledgement said "Thank God" and hung up. Only then did he tell me what was happening. He told me he had sent pilots in to bomb Hanoi Harbor. They had all returned alive. He could sleep now. I could go. We hugged. He fell to sleep around 4 A.M. The memory today of his angst and relief is as fresh as morning dew.

My father's final State of the Union speech was one of the last historic moments I witnessed. I took my eighteen-month-old son Lyndon with me; Daddy said he was the only person he was inviting. Everyone else in the family had thought it inappropriate to take my baby. I thought so too. But Daddy, forever the history teacher, wanted Lyndon to share in this historic moment even if he was too young to understand. Somehow, someway, baby Lyndon never offered a moment's disturbance, although he was awake the entire time. Somehow, someway, the Lord sends what you need to get through such moments of challenge in those hallowed halls.

What he sends that makes all the difference is the people. The domestic staff and administrative staff became my extended family. The White House domestic staff includes some of the world's great professionals. Many have served half a dozen presidential families. Yet they make every family feel they care most for them. When I left the White House, a wonderful maid, Clara, came to me crying. She was carrying a jar of formaldehyde with a cat fetus, from my nursing school days. She thrust it into my hands saying, "This is the only thing that I can think that is good about your leaving." No doubt I had presented all the staff some challenges, like when I lost my hamsters several days before Princess Margaret came for a state dinner. I may have challenged her, but Clara was always a loving, able presence in my life.

Like the domestic staff, the White House telephone operators are incredible, unsung heroes. They could find anybody in any part of the world seemingly instantly, and always without complaint. One of my favorite Christmas treats was taking the operators my homemade brownies. At least once a year I thanked the faces whose voices were constantly befriending me!

The staff on the east side and west side of the White House made me feel they were on my side almost all of the time. When they didn't, it was usually because I was shortsighted and wasn't looking at the most important part of the picture, my chance to serve. Usually Daddy brought all kinds of staff home to eat with us. We worked together, ate together, went to church together. We really lived together as family. Staff members' hopes and dreams were ours, and ours theirs.

Yes, life in the White House is like living in a goldfish bowl, always on display. But in fact it was the first time I remember actually eating dinner alone with my parents. Prior to the White House my parents were more often than not down at the Capitol until long past my bedtime. So when Daddy worked at home, as he did in the White House, I had the blissful experience of sometimes dining alone with them.

The lessons, the fears and tears of my times in the White House, were in many ways wasted on me, because I was so young. Too often I failed to treasure sufficiently the opportunities that were mine. But before it was all over, a far too early marriage, a husband at war, and a baby had matured me enough to recognize just how blessed I had been.

On January 20,1969, I stood on the edge of the inaugural platform after President Nixon had been inaugurated. I buried my head into the caring shoulder of a Secret Service man who had been with me all those years, just as I had done when the first one showed up on November 22, 1963. Both times, I was scared of the future. But my time in the White House had prepared me for all time to recognize that what happens to you doesn't matter nearly as much as how you handle it.

So what's the legacy from my White House days? It's a thousand friendships, a deep and abiding love of country and public service, a passion for learning, the recognition that the getting in life is truly to be found in the giving, and the belief that I should try to live each day as if it were my last. My life has been forever intellectually, emotionally, and spiritually enriched, because I was fortunate enough to be a resident of 1600 Pennsylvania Avenue. For every story of my White House days that I have shared here, there are dozens more.

And for each I am grateful.

In the pages that follow are the perceptions and remembrances of people who were deeply involved in my father's programs. Many were his close intimates during those critical years. They have recorded for posterity their thoughts and observations of his legacy, his programs, and our time together in the White House.

# Johnson in Literature and History

Lyndon Johnson, in the course of an interview with noted author Doris Kearns Goodwin, once remarked to her: ". . . there is no chance the ordinary person in the future will ever remember me. No chance," he said. "I'd rather have been better off looking for immortality through my wife and children and their children in turn instead of seeking all that love and affection from the American people. They're just too fickle." Professor Thomas W. Cowger examines the manner in which Johnson has been treated by writers and scholars, including those in the latest period of revisionism.

# They Will Never Remember Me: Johnson in Historical Literature
## Thomas W. Cowger

Lyndon Johnson once remarked to noted author Doris Kearns Goodwin in the course of an interview: ". . . There is no chance the ordinary person in the future will ever remember me. No chance," he said. "I'd rather have been better off looking for immortality through my wife and children and their children in turn instead of seeking all that love and affection from the American people. They're just too fickle."[1] Several decades later, Lyndon Johnson's skepticism proved unfounded, as most Americans, ranging from his most ardent supporters to his harshest critics, remember the thirty-sixth president's legacy and have an opinion about it. Moreover, from Johnson's White House years to the present, scholars and historians have debated and attempted to define his place in American history.

The earliest works detailing Johnson's political career were both partisan and nonobjective, largely written by Johnson's friends and associates, who heaped lavish praise on him. The first biography, *The Lyndon Johnson Story*, written by staff member Booth Moody in 1956 and later revised in 1964, was little more than propaganda designed to promote Johnson's rise to national prominence. Moody depicts Johnson as a thoughtful, upright, dispassionate, and patriotic activist. No mention is made by Moody of persistent charges levied against Johnson by some later authors, including character flaws, questionable means of amassing personal wealth, ties to wealthy powerful backers, or postwar abandonment of the New Deal programs he had so greatly admired in favor of the Taft-Hartley Act.[2]

Shortly after the assassination of President John F. Kennedy in 1963, *New York Times* journalist William S. White assured the downhearted and grieving American people that LBJ was more than up to the new challenge he faced as president. Johnson after all, according to White, had mastered the art of politics and had worked closely with both liberals and conservatives. White, a longtime friend of LBJ, declared that the former majority leader maintained a deep sense of southern and Texan humility.[3]

One year later, three historians at Southwest Texas State Teachers College, Johnson's alma matter, published an account of the president's childhood and early life in the hill country of Texas. William C. Pool, Emmie Craddock, and David C. Pool described Johnson as a progressive, grassroots politician blessed with the finest attributes of the Founding Fathers. Published in 1965, *Lyndon B. Johnson: The Formative Years* portrays the early influences that shaped a spirited, determined, and ambitious LBJ on his way to the presidency. As might be expected in a book written by his educational mentors, the most insightful discussions relate to Johnson's college years in San Marcos, Texas.[4]

Johnson's political adversaries wasted little time in answering these early pro-Johnson works. In 1964, J. Evetts Haley, an ultraconservative Texan, harshly and unfairly criticized the southern president. Insulted by the popular media portrayal of LBJ as a typical Texan, Haley viewed the new president as lacking strong, rooted Texas values and as an individual who came to power by happenstance, because of unusual historical circumstances. In *A Texan Looks at Lyndon: A Study in Illegitimate Power*, Haley chronicled what he perceived as the darker side of Johnson's rise to power. He charged Johnson with manipulating the 1948 Senate election to his advantage, with building his personal fortune by using the Federal Communications Commission to create a television monopoly in Texas, and with achieving political power by granting special privileges to powerful Texas business interests. Haley most harshly attacked LBJ's claims, as Senate majority leader in 1958, that he was bipartisan. Haley saw LBJ as an amoral political opportunist and manipulator, driven simply by the desire for wealth and power and lacking any ideological beliefs.[5]

Haley was not alone in his assaults on Johnson's alleged lack of guiding convictions. The president now came under attack from the opposite side of the political spectrum. In the turmoil of the late 1960s, Robert

Sherill, an ultraliberal, called Johnson a "welfare imperialist." Johnson, according to Sherill, had risen to power by accident and squandered one opportunity after another to make significant change in this country. In other words, power and wealth had driven LBJ, Sherill argued, not a deep commitment to help the disadvantaged and the under served. Thus, he owed his allegiance to the power brokers of Texas and not the people at large.[6]

One year later, journalist Alfred Steinberg published an unflattering biography of LBJ entitled *Sam Johnson's Boy: A Close-Up of the President from Texas*. In an extremely lengthy but unbalanced account, Steinberg attempted to validate the charges of improprieties raised earlier by Haley. Thus, he also saw Johnson as an opportunist guided by personal ambition. While Steinberg documented more fully than Haley some of LBJ's questionable Texas dealings, his personal biases against the president raise serious questions of objectivity and accuracy. Such personal biases led him to credit wrongly Senate majority leader Mike Mansfield with being the impetus for the Great Society programs and to question unfairly Johnson's motivations for civil rights legislation.

However, more importantly, Steinberg demonstrated how Johnson sought "political daddies" to adopt him as a protégé. These father figures ranged from Alvin Wirtz and Richard Russell to Sam Rayburn and Franklin D. Roosevelt. Each one helped groom and shape the young LBJ and opened political doors for him. Johnson, however, according to Steinberg, felt no long-term loyalties to his mentors and often abandoned them in pursuit of other political self-serving opportunities. Steinberg was the first critic to discuss fully the beliefs that shaped Johnson's views on foreign policy and defense spending. LBJ, Steinberg felt, having grown to adulthood in the 1930s during the rise of the Fascist and Nazi regimes, feared isolationism, weak defense, and passive foreign policy. Thus, he became a committed Cold Warrior who advocated heavy defense spending and militarism. His hawkish views, according to Steinberg, put him ultimately on a course to disaster, the tragedy in Vietnam.[7]

Within a short time after Steinberg's book, Sam Houston Johnson and Merle Miller took the opportunity to defend LBJ's reputation in *My Brother Lyndon* and *Lyndon, an Oral Biography*.[8] Sam Houston Johnson, the president's brother, blamed the Vietnam War not on his brother's hawkish views but instead on holdovers from the Kennedy administration who directed foreign policy. He argues that his brother often felt insecure around the well educated and seemingly more sophisticated Ivy

Leaguers. Although Sam Houston Johnson adored his brother, he acknowledged LBJ's temperamental and volatile nature. Miller for his part used transcripts from the LBJ library, interviews of his own, and personal observations to create his portrait of Johnson. Yet his work lacks critical analysis, and he failed to check his personal remembrances and square his sources with the documentary record. His account is unreliable in numerous places.[9]

In the decade of the 1970s, several former Johnson aides, and LBJ himself, took their turns detailing the Johnson presidency. Former LBJ aide George E. Reedy in 1970 took an oblique look at the Johnson presidency in his memoir *The Twilight of the Presidency*. Reedy argued that American presidents, like Johnson, lost touch with reality through official isolation.[10] In 1971, Johnson published *The Vantage Point*, described by the publisher as an intimate look at his presidential years. Several former White House aides, however, had largely written the account. They did the research and wrote the early drafts; Johnson made only the final revisions. The memoir is largely a lifeless record of official public policy, with few personal anecdotes, insights into, or "vantage points" on the making of history during these critical years.[11] The lengthy memoir defends Johnson's policies in Southeast Asia as an effort to stop the global advance of communism. In 1975, near America's bicentennial celebration, presidential aide Jack Valenti penned his own memoir, *A Very Human President*. His account is filled with unabashedly glowing praise for his former boss.[12]

Perhaps the most honest, balanced, and astute of the 1970s memoirs is Harry McPherson's *A Political Education*. A young Texan introduced to LBJ in 1956, McPherson later served as White House counsel and speechwriter. Johnson, he argued, taught him the nature of politics. McPherson ably described Johnson's skillful handling and manipulation of Congress in achieving his legislative agenda. While McPherson understood Johnson's flaws and limitations, he admired his talents and commitment to political ideology. He viewed Johnson as a national populist who opposed large corporations and deeply cared for the needs of the poor. Johnson's national movement failed, according to McPherson, because of his failure to communicate his message to the media, to the middle class in the southern and western parts of the United States, and to the dissatisfied youth of the 1960s. Johnson embraced militarism during the Cold War, he also notes, as the price the Democratic party had to pay to achieve social welfare successes in Congress.[13]

Few of Johnson's aides had closer relationships to the president than did Joseph Califano, his chief domestic policy adviser. Califano in 1991 detailed his service to LBJ in *The Triumph and Tragedy of Lyndon Johnson: The White House Years*.[14] Califano portrayed Johnson as "brave and brutal, compassionate and cruel, incredibly intelligent and infuriatingly insensitive."[15] This complicated personality, with its boundless energy, had mastered Washington politics, he explained, by controlling and dominating subordinates and associates. In particular, LBJ ignored the boundaries between public and private spaces—by placing associates in delicate situations, working them to exhaustion, and keeping them at his service twenty-four hours a day. While working with LBJ, Califano kept hundreds of pages of detailed notes from countless discussions with the president. He uses those sources in careful sketches of policymaking in the 1960s. Califano forces readers to reflect on what characteristics make for effective presidential leadership and to examine critically a political figure whose historical impact can hardly be overstated. Califano's account is at times personal, perceptive, moving, humorous, and somber.

Aside from the previously mentioned work by William S. White following Kennedy's assassination, other journalists also chronicled the Johnson presidency. Rowland Evans and Robert Novak, two well-known Washington figures, examined Johnson's political career in *Lyndon B. Johnson: The Exercise of Power*. Evans and Novak were the first to coin the expression the "Johnson treatment," which they described as a device used by LBJ to bully, cajole, persuade, and manipulate fellow politicians and aides into submission. They also aptly described the Johnson "network"—a group of diverse, bipartisan, loyal congressional officials upon whom Johnson could count for votes on the floor of Congress.[16]

As America became more deeply involved in Vietnam, two journalists attempted to explain Johnson's commitment to the war. Philip Geyelin in 1966 detailed Johnson's approach to foreign policy in *Lyndon B. Johnson and the World*. Geyelin saw LBJ as a self-taught foreign-policy specialist who relied on actions rather than words; he held that Johnson's view of previous U.S. foreign policy mistakes led him to overreact in Vietnam.[17] Tom Wicker, on the other hand, argued in 1968 in *JFK and LBJ* that Johnson's inexperience in foreign policy forced him to accept the Vietnam strategy he had inherited from John Kennedy.[18]

Several other reporters also searched for answers to explain the complex president. Jack Bell's *The Johnson Treatment*, Charles Robert's *LBJ's Inner Circle*, Frank Cormier's *LBJ: The Way He Was*, and Hugh

Sidey's *A Very Personal Presidency* looked at the multifaceted dimensions of LBJ's personality and attributed Johnson's failures to various personal shortcomings.[19] Richard Harwood and Haynes Johnson in *Lyndon*, written shortly after the president's death in 1973, in contrast, credited external forces outside LBJ's control with destroying any hope for success in pursuing his significant liberal impulses.[20] British journalist Louis Heren in *No Hail, No Farewell* objectively noted Johnson's personality imperfections as well as his unequaled political skills. Like Harwood and Johnson, Heren saw Johnson's demise as a result of circumstances outside his control. In particular, Johnson had attempted to apply liberal solutions dating back to Franklin D. Roosevelt to 1960s domestic and foreign problems that required more complex answers. In the end, in this view, Johnson lacked the political sophistication required to deal with the cultural revolution and massive social upheavals of the mid-to-late 1960s, problems that simply overwhelmed his leadership abilities and crippled his administration.[21]

In *The Politician*, Ronnie Dugger, the editor of the liberal *Texas Observer*, painted in 1982 a much less sympathetic portrait of Johnson than had most previous authors. Dugger found LBJ neither "tragic" nor worthy of adulation. Dugger blamed Johnson's failure to meet his liberal expectations on his rural upbringing in central Texas. Moreover, the president, according to Dugger, displayed unstable characteristics ranging from temperamental mood swings to potentially reckless and devastating fits of anger, fits that endangered all mankind. In Dugger's eyes, Johnson committed the ultimate, unforgivable act of irresponsibility by leading America headlong into the disaster in Vietnam. Thus, Dugger attempted to base all of LBJ's decisions on deep-rooted character flaws that had evolved from unmet childhood needs. In his narrow focus on theories about Johnson's personal behavior, however, Dugger failed to place LBJ in the larger historical context of his day and of the rapidly changing social and political world in which he lived.[22]

Following Dugger's account, Pulitzer Prize–winning journalist Robert Caro produced a best-selling study of LBJ. The first two volumes, *The Path to Power* and *Means of Ascent*, were in many ways more one-sided and critical than any previous work on the former president. Though his research was exhaustive, Caro unfortunately sometimes let his personal dislike for the president's flaws cloud his objectivity and scholarship. He appeared absolutely convinced that Johnson was a morally bankrupt and a fundamentally rotten person. Johnson, Caro argued, had been ruthlessly driven by an insatiable hunger for power and wealth and that he climbed the ladder of success through lies and corrupt practices. Moreover, Caro's belief that Johnson's craving for power and wealth and his assertive ego singularly drove all of LBJ's actions is too pat. Certainly, ideology and a sense of moral justice—loyalty to U.S. allies abroad, containment policy, racial, social, economic, legal equity, and understanding of the tenets of a good society—also informed his decisionmaking process and led him to champion numerous causes that were not political by expedient for him.[23] Recently, Caro produced a third volume, *Master of the Senate*. In this account, he details Johnson's twelve years in the Senate, from 1949 to 1960. In rich detail, Caro describes the inner workings of the Senate and how Johnson rose from relative obscurity to master that legislative body like no politician before or after him has done. This most recent product of Caro's lifelong work is nearly as long as his two previous works combined; it is also, perhaps, a little more balanced and objective than his first two books. Caro's next volume will detail the White House years.[24]

In recent decades, academically trained scholars have begun to weigh in on President Johnson's place in twentieth-century American history. Two Johnson insiders and trained scholars wrote some of the first scholarly accounts. A political historian and presidential assistant to LBJ, Eric F. Goldman, wrote *The Tragedy of Lyndon Johnson* in 1969. He describes in great detail the origins of the Great Society and Johnson's particular contributions to its legacy. Johnson's personal insecurities, Goldman maintained, forced him to seek the constant satisfaction and approval of the American people. In the end, LBJ never fully fulfilled the expectations of the urban middle class, which rejected him and many of his programs. Thus, he became a "tragic figure" whose well-intentioned efforts went unappreciated by the public and were lost in the unusual circumstances surrounding his time.[25]

One of the most intimate accounts of Lyndon Johnson's life came from Doris Kearns Goodwin, in *Lyndon Johnson and the American Dream*. The heart of her work is a series of extensive and highly personal interviews that she conducted with Johnson after he left office. Trained as a scholar and with experience as a White House aide to LBJ, Kearns Goodwin attempted to create a psychohistory of the president's life. The result is a unique, albeit controversial, portrait of the political career of Johnson.

According to Kearns Goodwin, the key to understanding the contradictions in Johnson's behavior is his relationship with his mother and father. While Johnson was growing up in central Texas, he faced conflicting pressures from his parents. Sam Johnson taught his young son the crude but exciting world of Texas politics. Sam, a respected U.S. representative from Texas, sometimes used offensive language, drank to excess, caroused late at night, and was prone to storytelling and occasional violent outbursts. He regularly subjected his son to tests of manliness. On the other hand, his mother, Rebekah, a refined and educated woman, instructed her son to value culture, idealism, and service. She invested all her hopes and dreams in Lyndon, Kearns Goodwin maintained, and withheld her love and affection from her son to force him to forsake his father's crude ways and adopt her genteel manner. These apparent contradictions in his life caused the young LBJ to seek in power, through public life, the approval his parents denied him at home. Torn by the inner struggles, LBJ turned to the manly world of politics, where he emulated his father's impulse toward manipulation, his colorful language, and his storytelling abilities, and also fulfilled his mother's goals of service and idealism by helping the disadvantaged.

The difficulty with Kearns Goodwin's psychological thesis is that it is almost impossible to test the accuracy of the information Johnson provided the young interviewer. Perhaps the material he provided Kearns Goodwin was little more than clouded memories, fabrications, or attempts to manipulate the final history of his life. Certainly, Johnson's version of events needs to be compared with information from other archival and published sources, and Kearns Goodwin's interpretations of those events need to be squared with other accounts.[26]

In 1981, two works came out that relied heavily on material contained at the Johnson presidential library in Austin, Texas. Emmette S. Redford and Marlan Blissett in *Organizing the Executive Branch: The Johnson Presidency* critically examined three major agencies: Housing and Urban Development, Department of Transportation, and the Office of Economic of Economic Opportunity. With funding from the National Endowment for the Humanities and using Johnson as a case study, the book traced the details of the managerial process involved at the executive level of American government.[27] Distinguished University of Texas professor Robert A. Divine also edited a collection of eight essays collectively entitled *Exploring the Johnson Years*. Ranging from the War on Poverty to the war in Vietnam, these essays described the holdings in the LBJ library on a broad range of topics. Scholars and graduate students continue to mine this reference for useful documents and insights into the Johnson years.[28]

Vaughn Davis Bornet, author of works on welfare, labor, and Herbert Hoover, examined in 1983 the presidency of Lyndon Johnson. His work is not biographical, focusing more on Johnson's administration than on the president himself. Bornet applauded LBJ's lofty goals—his commitment to civil rights, education, medical care, housing, the environment, and overall improvement in the quality of American life. Yet he faulted Johnson for trying to promise, and ultimately achieve, too much through his Great Society and War on Poverty programs and the war in Vietnam. LBJ attempted, according to Bornet, to accomplish more than most Americans were willing to support, and these unrealistic expectations produced problems that linger today.[29]

In contrast, Allen J. Matusow, the author of several studies, examined the next year the history of Kennedy-Johnson liberalism.[30] Primarily concerned with domestic policies, he traced Johnson's liberal acquisition, use, and ultimate loss of power. In a bold and clear writing style, Matusow blamed liberalism's failure in the 1960s on the "softness" of the liberal reformers who promoted change. In other words, they underestimated the complexities of the obstacles they faced as well as failed to understand fully their own proposed solutions to those problems. Moreover, they did not challenge the existing distribution of power in America but instead wrongly compromised with corporations, political power brokers, and other special interest groups to defeat any opportunities for significant change. The War on Poverty, Matusow contends, produced "one of the greatest failures of twentieth century liberalism."[31] In the end, the inability of liberals to achieve lasting change and the rejection of liberalism by middle-class Americans in 1968 launched the beginnings of the later conservative ascendance.

Two years later, noted historian Paul Conkin wrote a concise and thoughtful one-volume biography of LBJ.[32] While offering little in the way of new interpretation, Conklin masterfully corrected the exaggerations of earlier Johnson biographers and offered a readable, balanced treatment of his subject. Unlike Dugger and Caro, who saw Johnson as a man driven by an insatiable appetite for power and control, Conkin portrayed him as a complex figure capable of a full range of emotions: generosity, sincerity, insecurity, egotism, and manipulation. In the process, Conkin subtly cast doubts on the reliability of some of Caro's sources relating to Johnson's early life. Conkin praised Johnson's civil rights efforts but found his antipoverty programs lacking direction and falling short of their lofty goals. Johnson, according to Conkin, failed to recognize the inherent limits of the federal government's ability to solve social problems, for which reason his initiatives sometimes produced the opposite of the desired effect. In the end, Conklin believed, Johnson proved unable to see "how even the best-laid plans go awry, of how often the consequences of human choice are the very opposite of what one intended, of how unknown complications always lurk and often doom our best-intentioned efforts."[33] Inherited foreign policies also held LBJ captive in Vietnam. Thus, the failures in Vietnam and at home led the "Big Daddy" from the hill country region to die brokenhearted, never having fully won the public love he so desperately craved.

The decade of the 1990s produced a flurry of new works of the Johnson years. Paul Henggeler devoted a whole book to the relationship between LBJ and JFK and its subsequent effect on the Johnson presidency. *In His Steps* argues that LBJ used, and in some sense contributed to, the myth of Kennedy to enact the Great Society and escalate the war in Vietnam. Writing in 1991, Henggeler also maintained that while the Kennedy legacy served him well it also hamstrung him, because the policies and personnel that Johnson inherited from the martyred president prevented him from creating his own staff and forging his own programs and legacy. Thus, ironically, Kennedy contributed to both Johnson's successes and his failures. Henggeler also in copious detail examined the bitter feud between Johnson and Robert Kennedy.[34]

Two recent scholars have looked closely at the legacy of the Great Society. In *From Opportunity to Entitlement: The Transformation and Decline of Great Society Liberalism*, Gareth Davies attempts to explain the collapse of the New Deal coalition and the recent resurgence of American conservatism. Davies believes that Johnson liberals abandoned a strategy of "opportunity" (self-help assistance) liberalism to fight poverty in favor of entitlement (income assistance) liberalism. Following the race riots of the mid-1960s and loss of credibility in Vietnam, congressional liberals embraced guaranteed income as a right of poor persons. This change in policy violated traditional values of individualism and alienated middle-class Americans, who then abandoned Great Society programs.[35] John A. Andrews III set out to write in 1998 a fair and balanced assessment of Great Society legislation. Examining the programs that failed, he notes that such measures suffered as civil rights activism and urban riots increasingly alarmed white America, and that initiatives like the Department of Housing and Urban Development lacked federal regulation and adequate funding. Yet he records lasting successes in such measures as beautification projects, consumer rights legislation, and crime control laws.[36]

Renowned historian Irving Bernstein, in a highly readable narrative, recently attempted to restore Johnson's place in modern American history. In *Guns and Butter: The Presidency of Lyndon Johnson*, Berstein offers a skillful assessment of Johnson's successes and failures, from legislative programs to a futile war in Vietnam, to his failure to promote Hubert Humphrey's presidential campaign in 1968. The Great Society, he concludes, succeeded. Yet it did not live up to its full potential, because Johnson attempted to have both "guns and butter"—massive domestic measures alongside an unpopular, undeclared war in Southeast Asia. Ultimately, the conflict in Vietnam led to increased federal spending and runaway inflation that undermined the Johnson presidency and produced a tragedy of epic proportions.[37]

In *Mutual Contempt*, Jeff Shesol, a former Rhodes scholar and creator of the nationally syndicated political comic strip *Thatch*, presented in 1997 the first full-length study of the antipathy between two of the 1960s most powerful political figures, Johnson and Robert Kennedy. Ironically, both of these men had laid claim to the Camelot legacy, but neither trusted or liked the other. The feud began with Robert Kennedy's opposition to the selection of Johnson as his brother's running mate in 1960. It continued during the Kennedy presidency, as Robert Kennedy attempted to ignore Johnson or exclude him from any role in the administration. After John Kennedy's assassination in 1963, LBJ distanced himself from Robert Kennedy and denied him a role in his presidency. In particular, Johnson refused to select Kennedy as his vice-presidential running mate in 1964. As the social turmoil of the late 1960s intensified, Johnson, according to Shesol, became increasingly more distrustful of Robert Kennedy and blamed many of his difficulties on this adversary. He specifically detested Kennedy's antiwar platform and aspirations for the presidency. Paradoxically, the men differed little on issues other than Vietnam. Their mutual scorn ended only with Robert Kennedy's death in 1968. By that time, Johnson had announced he would not seek reelection, and his political career and tragic presidency was coming to an end.[38]

Writing on the heels of the Newt Gingrich-led Republican revolution in 1994, Pulitzer Prize–winning historian Irwin Unger and his wife, in a pair of books, analyzed LBJ and his Great Society. In *The Best of Intentions*, Irwin Unger scrutinized the successes and failures of Great Society legislation under the three 1960s presidents. Believing Johnson sincere in his efforts to help the under served, Unger demonstrates how the credibility gap, riots in the cities, and an economic recession destroyed the well-intentioned war on poverty. He concedes that many of Johnson's domestic programs failed, but he finds success in such programs as health, education, public broadcasting, consumer and environmental protection, national endowments in the arts and humanities, billboard removal, and expanded national parks. More recently, Irwin and Debi Unger teamed up to write *LBJ: A Life*. While the biography offers few new insights into Johnson's life, it does present a good introduction to its subject.[39]

Without question, some of the best scholarship on Johnson and his presidency has come in recent years. The two-volume biographical contribution of Robert Dallek is an example. In *Lone Star Rising and Flawed Giant*, Dallek has produced the most thoughtful, comprehensive, balanced, and reliable account of the thirty-sixth president's life. Dallek rises above the earlier regional and political biases that so often marked earlier writings on Johnson, presenting LBJ in the context of his times and relating him to the larger themes and questions of the twentieth century. Moreover, he portrays Johnson with his blemishes and warts alongside his admirable traits and attributes. Through Dallek's eyes, the reader sees an individual capable of crudeness, self-interest, and vindictiveness who also demonstrated political savvy, sincere concern for the disadvantaged, kindness for little political advantage, and a tireless energy as a public servant. Johnson, according to Dallek, represented a "liberal nationalist" dedicated to the belief in federal intervention to solve society's greatest challenges. Dallek traces in exhaustive detail Johnson's rise to national prominence, his legislative triumphs in the Great Society, his catastrophe in Vietnam, and his lonely death.[40]

Thus after nearly thirty years of repudiation, the historiographical view LBJ and his place in American history is being greatly revised, and he is gaining favor in many circles. Not long ago, George McGovern, antiwar presidential nominee in 1972, suggested in the *New York Times* that aside from Woodrow Wilson and the two Roosevelts, Johnson was the most important president since Abraham Lincoln. The noted economist John Kenneth Galbraith, a longtime critic of Johnson, also recently acknowledged the importance of LBJ's place in the twentieth century.[41] Others have followed suit. As Lewis Gold notes in one of the most recent issues of the *Wilson Quarterly*, "Vice President [Al] Gore has listed Johnson among the presidents he most admires. *Boston Globe* columnist David Shribman calls LBJ 'the hottest political figure in the nation right now.' In the academy and the political arena alike, there is renewed interest in the large visions that drove Lyndon Johnson and a fresh desire to modify the historical picture of his presidency."[42] Another reflection of Johnson's revised image is that not long ago a panel of fifty-eight historians assembled by C-SPAN ranked him tenth best among America's forty-one presidents.[43]

The resurrection of Johnson's reputation is due in part to the passage of time, but more importantly to a decision by Harry Middleton, director of the LBJ library, to open to the public an extensive collection of secret recordings of Johnson's telephone conversations in the White House. Middleton has been credited as "the man who saved LBJ" and as having set off a wave of revisionist history.[44] President Johnson had not wanted the tapes released until fifty years after his death, but the 1993 decision allowed scholars, researchers, and the general public to see the human and candid side of the masterful politician and to reassess their opinions of him. In other words, it has allowed a new generation of listening audiences the opportunity to sit on the historical jury. Among other things, the tapes shift some of the emphasis on Vietnam away from Johnson and point to relentless pressure exerted by the U.S. military and CIA for wider American intervention. They also show a president deeply committed to social issues. Excerpts reproduced by historian Michael Beschloss in *Taking Charge: The Johnson White House Tapes, 1936–1964* further brought the very human and uncensored LBJ into the homes of the American people.[45]

LBJ never believed, as Doris Kearns Goodwin noted, that historians and the general public would give him a fair shake. The passage of time has proved him wrong. From his last days in the White House in 1968 until the present, numerous works have been written about him and his administration. Moreover, new books are appearing on bookstore and library shelves all the time. No doubt he would be greatly pleased with his political rebirth and the heightened scholarly and public interest in him and his programs.

## Notes

1. Doris Kearns Goodwin, *Lyndon Johnson and the American Dream* (New York: Harper and Row, 1976; reprinted New York: St. Martin Press, 1991), i.

2. Booth Mooney, *The Lyndon Johnson Story* (New York: Farrar, Straus and Cudahy, 1956).

3. William S. White, *The Professional: Lyndon B. Johnson* (Boston: Houghton Mifflin, 1964).

4. William C. Pool, Emmie Cradduck, and David Conrad, *Lyndon Baines Johnson: The Formative Years* (San Marcos: Southwest Texas State College Press, 1965).

5. J. Evetts Haley, *A Texan Looks at Lyndon: A Study in Illegitimate Power* (Canyon, Tex.: Palo Duro Press, 1964).

6. Robert Sherill, *Accidental President* (New York: Grossman, 1967).

7. Alfred Steinberg, *Sam Johnson's Boy: A Close-Up of the President from Texas* (New York: Macmillan, 1968).

8. Sam Houston Johnson, *My Brother Lyndon* (New York: Cowles, 1969).

9. Merle Miller, *Lyndon: An Oral Biography* (New York: Ballantine Press, 1980).

10. George E. Reedy, *The Twilight of the Presidency* (New York: World, 1970).

11. Lyndon Baines Johnson, *The Vantage Point: Perspectives of the Presidency, 1963–1969* (New York: Holt, Rinehart and Winston, 1971).

12. Jack Valenti, *A Very Human President* (New York: W. W. Norton, 1975).

13. Harry McPherson, *A Political Education* (Boston: Little, Brown, 1972).

14. Joseph A. Califano, Jr., *The Triumph and Tragedy of Lyndon Johnson: The White House Years* (New York: Simon & Schuster, 1991).

15. Califano, *The Triumph and Tragedy of Lyndon Johnson*, 10.

16. Rowland Evans and Robert Novak, *Lyndon B. Johnson: The Exercise of Power* (New York: New American Library, 1966).

17. Philip Geyelin, *Lyndon Johnson and the World* (New York: Praeger, 1966).

18. Tom Wicker, *JFK and LBJ: The Influence of Personality upon Politics* (New York: William Morrow, 1968).

19. Jack Bell, *The Johnson Treatment: How Lyndon B. Johnson Took Over the Presidency and Made It His Own* (New York: Harper and Row, 1965); Charles Roberts, *LBJ's Inner Circle* (New York: Delacorte Press, 1965): Frank Cormier, *LBJ: The Way He Was* (New York: Doubleday, 1977); and Hugh Sidey, *A Very Personal Presidency: Lyndon Johnson in the White House* (New York: Atheneum, 1968).

20. Richard Harwood and Haynes Johnson, *Lyndon* (New York: Praeger, 1973).

21. Louis Heren, *No Hail, No Farewell* (New York: Harper and Row, 1970).

22. Ronnie Dugger, *The Politician: The Life and Times of Lyndon Johnson* (New York: W. W. Norton, 1982).

23. Robert Caro, *The Years of Lyndon Johnson: The Path to Power* (New York: Alfred A. Knopf, 1982), and *The Years of Lyndon Johnson: Means of Ascent* (New York: Alfred A. Knopf, 1990).

24. Robert Caro, *Master of the Senate: The Years of Lyndon Johnson* (New York: Alfred A. Knopf, 2002).

25. Eric F. Goldman, *The Tragedy of Lyndon Johnson* (New York: Alfred A. Knopf, 1969).

26. Kearns Goodwin, *Lyndon Johnson and the American Dream*.

27. Emmette S. Redford and Marlan Lissett, *Organizing the Executive Branch: The Johnson Presidency* (Chicago: University of Chicago Press, 1981).

28. Robert A. Divine, ed., *Exploring the Johnson Years* (Austin: University of Texas Press, 1981).

29. Vaughn Davis Bornet, *The Presidency of Lyndon Johnson* (Lawrence: University of Kansas Press, 1983).

30. Allen J. Matusow, *The Unraveling of America: A History of Liberalism in the 1960s* (New York: Harper Torchbooks, 1984).

31. Matusow, *The Unraveling of America*, 220.

32. Paul Conkin, *Big Daddy from the Pedernales: Lyndon Baines Johnson* (Boston: Twayne, 1986).

33. Conkin, *Big Daddy from the Pedernales*, 237.

34. Paul R. Henggeler, *In His Steps: Lyndon Johnson and the Kennedy Mystique* (Chicago: Ivan R. Dee, 1991).

35. Gareth Davies, *From Opportunity to Entitlement: The Transformation and Decline of Great Society Liberalism* (Lawrence: University of Kansas Press, 1996).

36. John A. Andrew III, *Lyndon Johnson and the Great Society* (Chicago: Ivan R. Dee, 1998).

37. Irving Bernstein, *Guns or Butter: The Presidency of Lyndon Johnson* (New York: Oxford University Press, 1996).

38. Jeff Shesol, *Mutual Contempt: Robert Kennedy, and the Feud That Defined a Decade* (New York: W. W. Norton, 1997).

39. Irwin Unger, *The Best of Intentions: The Triumph and Failures of the Great Society under Kennedy, Johnson and Nixon* (New York: Doubleday, 1996); Irwin and Debi Unger, *LBJ: A Life* (New York: John Wiley, 1999).

40. Robert Dallek, *Lone Star Rising: Lyndon Johnson and His Times, 1908–1960* (New York: Oxford University Press, 1991), and *Flawed Giant: Lyndon Johnson and His Times, 1961–1973* (New York: Oxford University Press, 1998).

41. Lewis L. Gould, "The Revised LBJ," *Wilson Quarterly* 24 (Spring 2000): 80–83.

42. Gould, "The Revised LBJ," 80.

43. Paul Burka, "The Man Who Saved LBJ," *Texas Monthly* 28 (August 2000): 118–21.

44. Burka, "The Man Who Saved LBJ."

45. Michael R. Beschloss, ed., *Taking Charge: The Johnson White House Tapes, 1963–64* (New York: Simon & Schuster, 1997).

# SECTION TWO

# Tall Texan in a Stetson:
# Johnson's Personality

Without question, Lyndon Johnson was a complex individual, with an often contradictory personality. He has been variously described as mean-
spirited and petty, manipulative and condescending, micromanaging and
Machiavellian, and as visionary and idealistic, benevolent and sensitive,
charismatic and inspiring. Air Force general James Cross, Jack Valenti,
and Sherwin J. Markman attempt to reconcile those differences and paint
a more balanced portrait of Johnson the man and Johnson the president.
In the process, they force the reader to consider some critical questions.
How much in Johnson's programs was a product of him personally
and how much was it the personalities of his staff members and appointees? Viewed another way, was he simply a product of his times, or
was he a truly unique visionary, the likes of which we may never again see
in the presidency?

# An Uncommon, Common Man: LBJ's Pilot Remembers Him
## James Cross

How did someone raised on a farm in southern Alabama come to be command pilot for a vice president, later a president, and finally find himself as armed forces aide to the thirty-sixth president of the United States? Happenstance perhaps?

Having flown heavy transport aircraft for Troop Carrier Command and the Military Air Transport Service (MATS) for almost fifteen years, I was reassigned by the Air Force Personnel service in 1958 to the Special Air Missions unit in Washington, D.C. The unit is sometimes referred to as the "VIP Wing." At the time I was vaguely aware of Lyndon Baines Johnson's status as majority leader of the Senate, but I knew nothing of his background, his politics, or his personality. I did understand he was authorized to travel on, and frequently used, special missions aircraft when on official business related to military activities.

Upon arrival in Washington, each new assignee to the unit was always welcomed and indoctrinated by an appointed sponsor. One of the very first things I learned from mine was that if you ever get a mission as pilot for LBJ be very, very careful, because he has an explosive temper, doesn't suffer fools lightly, and can ruin your Air Force career if you fail to do things exactly as he expects. I stored that bit of advice for future reference, but my first encounter with him didn't come about until December 1961, after he had been elected vice president.

The Special Air Missions unit had just been reequipped with a new-type aircraft, the Lockheed Jetstar. The craft was a four-engine executive plane capable of carrying a crew of four and from eight to thirteen passengers, depending on the interior configuration. My role at that point in time as unit chief pilot resulted in my being the first to be certified as mission ready, thus I found myself assigned as pilot for Johnson's first Jetstar trip. I prepared for the flight with considerable misgivings.

The mission—first to Chicago, on the ground for a couple of hours, then on to his ranch at Stonewall, Texas—was anything but routine. The weather was stormy and turbulent, and we had in-flight weather delays at both destinations. I thought it was a terrible trip, but when he got off at his ranch he smiled and said, "Major, that was a really nice trip. You seem like a can-do man." I was greatly relieved as he went on to say, "I want you to come back next week for me, as I will need to get back to Washington."

However, the operations dispatcher normally assigns flight crews for the missions on a first-in, first-out basis, so my next encounter with him did not occur until early January 1962. He was to be picked up in Texas and flown to Palm Beach, Florida. There he would have meetings with President Kennedy, members of the cabinet, and the congressional leadership in preparation for the reconvening of Congress a day or so later in Washington.

Arriving at Bergstrom Air Force Base, near Austin, Texas, on the appointed morning, I telephoned him at his ranch. He immediately wanted to know what I was doing at Bergstrom. He said he wanted to leave from his ranch airstrip and that I should bring the plane to that location. As tactfully as I could, I informed him that we couldn't leave from his ranch, because the runway was too short for takeoff with the fuel load we would require for a nonstop flight to Palm Beach. His reply was an LBJ classic—"I'll be damned if I know why it is that you air force people can always figure out some way to mess up my plans." Without waiting for an answer, he asked about the enroute weather, how long it would take to make the flight, and what time we would need to leave Bergstrom AFB to reach Palm Beach at 3:55 P.M. Eastern Standard Time. He insisted that we make it on time, because a plane carrying cabinet officers and congressional leaders would be arriving in Palm Beach from Washington, D.C., at 4 P.M. President Kennedy would be at the airport to meet the delegation, and LBJ wanted to be there a minute or so ahead of him. My reply to his questions was, "Two hours and twenty five minutes, Mr. Vice President. We must leave Bergstrom at 12:30 P.M. due to the one-hour time-zone difference." Well, the morning wore on, and 12:30 came and went. At 12:45 an operations officer came from the air terminal and told me "the vice president is on his car radiophone and wants to talk with you." With mounting concern, I ran to speak with him, and he said, "Major, this is Lyndon Johnson. What time do I have to leave Bergstrom to arrive in Florida before 4 P.M.?" I looked at my watch and it showed 12:50. Using all the tact I could muster, I told him it would be particularly difficult to make the 3:55 time, since we really should have been airborne at 12:30. I then asked where he was at that moment. He responded that he was in Oak Hill on US Highway 290 driving ninety miles an hour. Oak Hill happens to be a small bedroom community about ten miles west of Austin, and a good twenty to thirty minutes' driving time from Bergstrom Air Force Base. When the conversation ended, I walked back across the ramp in a dejected frame of mind, expecting another twenty minutes or so of delay. But by the time I got back to the plane he was roaring up, driving himself in his Lincoln convertible, with no Secret Service personnel in attendance. I could only suppose that his earlier remark about his location and speed in Oak Hill had been meant to convey to me a particular sense of urgency.

His ruse, if that's what it was, worked. We changed our flight plan as soon as we were airborne, put the plane up to its maximum cruise speed (about sixty miles per hour faster than normal cruise), flew a direct path to Palm Beach, and made it just ahead of the Washington plane and a moment or so before the president. Incidentally, he too was driving his own Lincoln convertible.

The following day, when the vice president returned to the airport to be flown back to Washington, he gave me the well-chronicled and classic LBJ treatment. Grasping my coat lapels, he pulled me to within a few inches of his face and said, "Major, I don't know whether you will appreciate this or not but I told Secretary of Defense Robert McNamara last night that you were a can-do man and that I wanted him to see to it that you are appointed as my regular and permanent pilot." Thereafter for the next eleven years, until his death in January 1973, I was privileged to enjoy a close relationship with him and honored to serve him and his family.

In the early months of my association with LBJ, I began to feel that he was restless and unfulfilled in his role as vice president. On the occasion of Mrs. Eleanor Roosevelt's death he called to inform me that he would attend the funeral. Additionally, he asked that I arrange to land his plane at an airfield near the Roosevelt estate at Hyde Park, New York, but that I avoid landing at West Point, since President Kennedy's plane would be stopping there for the funeral. With air traffic control authorities required to give air priority to the presidential aircraft, Johnson was concerned that once the ceremony for Mrs. Roosevelt concluded, presidential prerogatives would kick in and delay his own immediate departure for an especially important appointment back in Washington. Accordingly, in concert with federal aviation officials and in keeping with his wishes, I made arrangements to use the Poughkeepsie, New York, airport as the landing site.

Best-laid plans sometimes go awry, and our departure back to Washington was delayed anyway. While we were awaiting takeoff clearance on the Poughkeepsie runway, LBJ sent for me to come back to the passenger cabin. He was, in a word, furious. He began by upbraiding me about the weather and wondered why a vice president of the United States couldn't get some priority, particularly since we had selected a landing site some distance from the president's location at West Point. Annoyed by the seemingly interminable delay, he complained, "Why in the hell couldn't the air traffic control system let the president's plane take off in a westerly direction, my own plane to the east, then vector us both back toward Washington at different altitudes?" That was certainly a legitimate argument, but I could only offer agreement and sympathy.

As his angst began to subside he talked about his role as vice president and wondered aloud why he had ever accepted the nomination in the first place. He said he didn't really need the hassle of public service any longer, since Mrs. Johnson owned a TV and radio station in Austin and they had sufficient income to live and support their family. Then his face softened, and his countenance lit up as he began to enthuse about his ranch in Texas and how much he loved the land, his heritage, and his family. He concluded with the comment that when his term as vice president was up he would just quit Washington and go back to his beloved hill country, since he wasn't appreciated in Washington anymore, anyway. Shortly, a crewman came and notified me that we had received clearance for takeoff, and my presence in the cockpit was expected.

The ensuing months were busy but pretty much routine. Then came President Kennedy's assassination in Dallas in November 1963. Several days later at the LBJ Ranch, the president told me that I was to continue flying his Jetstar but that I should also become qualified in the larger Boeing 707, which was the number-one presidential aircraft, usually known to the public as "Air Force One." Actually, the term applies to any air force aircraft in which the president is flying. If he is flying in a Marine Corps craft, such as a presidential helicopter, it is referred to as "Marine One."

After Johnson accepted the Democratic nomination in August 1964, his travel pace picked up dramatically, lasting throughout the campaign until we landed back in Austin on election day. Earlier that day the president's military aide, General Chester Clifton, informed us air force folk that we were to stay alert and close at hand even though the president had indicated he would use army helicopter transportation to return to his ranch later that night after the election results were in. A storm front came through the area around 9 P.M., however, so the helicopters were grounded. Some time later, around 11 P.M., the president's enlisted aide, Master Sergeant Paul Glynn, woke me from a sound sleep in my hotel room with the news that the president was on his way to Bergstrom field expecting me to fly him home to his ranch in the Jetstar. Arriving half-dressed and just moments before LBJ, we successfully circumnavigated the storm for a safe landing at his ranch. The following morning he informed me that henceforth, whenever he was in residence at the ranch, he expected me to keep the Jetstar on alert status there, at all times. Previously, while serving as vice president, and later as he finished the remainder of President Kennedy's term, he had specifically directed that we not stay at the ranch.

In late June 1965, word reached the Pentagon that General Clifton, who had served as military aide to President Kennedy and had remained in that position with President Johnson, would retire from the army. To my total surprise, a few days later, on July 10, the president nominated me to replace the general. He had not mentioned a word to me or even given a clue as to his intentions, and for two or three subsequent days he did not bother to enlighten me about his decision. Finally, the following week, he buttonholed me with this observation: "Major, you were here for us at planting time and I thought you ought to be around for the harvest. I want you to accomplish two things during your tenure as military aide. First, you've got a terrible mess in that military office in the East Wing. I want you to straighten it out and keep it straight. You've got 2,000 military people over there, all of them out giving press interviews and advertising that they work for the president. This president doesn't know who they are or what they do, and I don't need them. I'll give you six months to get rid of half your people, and if you can't do the job I'll find someone who can. In the meantime, don't be holding any press conferences, don't fire anybody, and don't make anybody mad. Just get rid of them."

A few days later, after completing an audit of the people that were assigned to the military office, I found that there were actually just a few in excess of 1,100 military personnel. They were handling such chores as the White House motor pool, helicopter operations, staff dining room, operating and maintaining Camp David, and manning and operating a naval squadron responsible for the presidential yachts. Additionally, there was a classified caretaker and operating group of specialists responsible for around-the-clock readiness of hardened and secure underground facilities that had been provided for continuation of the government in the event of an attack by enemies of the United States. While we weren't able to reduce the staff by half as he had directed, we were able to reduce the number to 587 people within the specified time. I seriously doubt that the task was accomplished without upsetting more than a few people.

The president also told me, in his own inimitable style, that he didn't think the military assistant had much responsibility, so I wouldn't have a great deal to do. Therefore he expected me to continue as command pilot for both the Jetstar and the Boeing 707. Never at a loss for a thoughtful rejoinder, my response was, of course, "Yes Sir!"

Within a few days he had surprised me—as well as military authorities in the Pentagon—out of our collective wits with my appointment as armed forces aide. Press coverage of the announcement elicited a few uncomplimentary remarks from some Pentagon wannabes who apparently lusted after General Clifton's job. Accordingly, print press operatives picked it up, and a couple of news publications published articles that were less than complimentary about my qualifications to be the president's aide, and equally tweaking the president for selecting someone for the position without a blue-blood pedigree or Rhodes Scholarship background. Within a few days the president intercepted me near the Rose Garden and asked, "Cross, what are you going to do about all your friends in the Pentagon talking out of school and saying bad things about you to the press?" I responded that I was certainly sorry that such talk might be reflecting on his stewardship of the presidency but that I didn't have any real friends in the Pentagon, and in any event, I was powerless to control anything coming from there. He said, "Well somebody ought to shut them up." This little scenario played itself out at the LBJ Ranch a couple of weeks later.

With the president resting at his home, Secretary McNamara flew in one evening to join him for a day or so. Early the next morning I carried the president a rather important top-secret message that had just arrived by teletype. Finding him and McNamara relaxing in the swimming pool, I apologized for interrupting, handed the president a towel and his glasses, and stood by while he read the message in case he wished to take any follow-up action. After reading the document he passed it to McNamara, commenting, "What do you think of this Bob?" After they talked about the message a moment or so, I figured I wasn't needed any longer, so I started to leave. The president then said, "By the way, Bob, do you know Major Cross?" (LBJ had first known me as a major, and although over the years he saw to it that I was advanced to the rank of brigadier general, I think he enjoyed devilishly needling me from time to time by referring to me as a major or calling me "Major" right up to the date of his death.) McNamara, being a very proper politician replied, "Oh yes, Mr. President, I know the colonel." Actually, I had only met McNamara a few days earlier. The president continued, "You know Bob, some of your Pentagon people have been talking to the press and questioning the president's judgment for appointing Cross to be military assistant. They have intimated that he doesn't have the experience, the background, or the education to handle that kind of responsibility. Now I know he didn't graduate cum laude from one of those elite eastern universities like Yale or Princeton—he went to some little old cow college in Alabama, I think—but I'll tell you one thing, Bob, he is loyal. And if I have a choice, when selecting someone to work for me, between a loyal, old, dumb country boy like Cross or a Ph.D. scholar from Harvard who has his own agenda, then I will pick the old country boy every time. Now Bob, you see if you can't stop this talk coming out of the Pentagon about poor old Cross." That backhanded vote of confidence sustained me throughout the rest of his presidency and later retirement.

A flying trip to Asian countries a few days before the congressional elections in 1966 enabled the president to have summit meetings with government leaders in New Zealand, Australia, the Philippines, Thailand, Malaysia, and South Korea. But in my opinion, a carefully scripted secret side trip to South Vietnam became the highlight of the entire trip for him. During a lull in his official agenda while in Manila, the president called me and asked that I move Air Force One to a nearby airport away from Manila International, cautioning me to take care that press representatives not learn of the move. The nearest suitable airport was the American naval air station at Sangley Point, across the bay from Manila. It was nonetheless near enough that presidential helicopters could reach it. While naval commanders at the base were still wondering why the presidential aircraft had landed at Sangley Point (I told them we were test-flying the plane after maintenance), LBJ arrived by helicopter in his ranch khakis, and off we flew to a warm reception with the troops at Cam Ranh Bay, South Vietnam. The Washington press corps was incensed at having been left behind for the event.

Later, during an April 1967 summit meeting with Latin American leaders in Punta del Este, Uruguay, President Johnson received word of the death of Konrad Adenauer, a former chancellor of West Germany. The evening before leaving Uruguay to return to the States, he advised me to begin making the necessary logistical arrangements for travel to Germany for the Adenauer funeral. After he took a brief, one-day rest at his ranch while the rites were being finalized, we departed on Air Force One for the long journey to Bonn, on April 23, 1967.

As a measure of LBJ's compassion, at a private birthday dinner arranged at the American embassy in Bonn for my forty-second birthday, he remembered a friend in Stonewall, Texas, who had been born and raised in Germany. Father Wunibald Schneider, the priest at the little Stonewall Catholic Church, hadn't been home in years. The president asked me to see if any air force planes might be leaving the States for Germany in the next few days and, if so, whether we could make arrangements to get Father Schneider a seat. Luckily the commander of SHAPE (Supreme Headquarters Allied Powers Europe), General Lyman L. Lemnitzer, was in Washington and would soon return to Europe. The presidential Jetstar was still at the Stonewall Ranch, momentarily due to return to Washington with an open seat. I was able to make arrangements by phone for Father Schneider to fly to Washington on the Jetstar and link up with General Lemnitzer's plane the next morning. I felt privileged to meet Father Schneider on behalf of the president with a staff car and send him on his way to his extended family in his ancestral homeland.

The drowning death in mid-December 1967 of Australia's Prime Minister Harold Holt afforded an opportunity for us to observe an especially broad range of the LBJ persona. Just minutes after the news flash came through wire services, the president called and asked if I had heard. I responded affirmatively. He indicated that he would be going to the funeral and that I should make arrangements to get his big plane ready to leave the next day. He wanted to know how long it would take for us to get there, whether we could go nonstop from Washington (we couldn't), and what the weather conditions would be for the trip. He told me that he would be taking some guests, gave me their names, and asked me to make arrangements to locate them and make sure they were aboard the plane in time for the departure. Lastly, he admonished me to be sure there was plenty of good food and drink on board, especially diet Fresca. He was a great fan of Fresca.

At that point in the conversation, I reluctantly reminded him of a conversation we had at his ranch a few weeks earlier. I had informed him of, and he had approved, plans to send the principal presidential aircraft for its biennial overhaul. I told him the plane had been flown to the overhaul facility in New York about ten days earlier, thus would be pretty well dismantled by now. Without pausing, he said, "That's alright. Just call them up, tell them to put it back together and you can go up this afternoon and bring it back so we can leave tomorrow." I told him the plane would not be flyable again for at least another forty-five days. His discomfort index soared when I shared that bit of news with him. However, we were able to make some modifications to one of our backup 707 airplanes and leave Washington on the 19th of December. None of the backup planes were quite as comfortable as the primary aircraft, nor did they have its extended range. Refueling stops were therefore necessary at Travis Air Force Base in California, at Honolulu, and in American Samoa. We arrived safely at Canberra some twenty-seven elapsed hours later (that is, counting time-zone changes).

After the Holt memorial service the following day in Melbourne, the president's agenda included a stop at Korat Royal Thai Air Base in Thailand, where he visited with some American crewmen who were flying bombing missions into North Vietnam. A quick turnaround back to the south and east brought us to Cam Ranh Bay in South Vietnam, where he would speak with and enjoy the company of a large group of service men and women who had been assembled to see and hear their president.

Then, instead of returning directly to the United States, as almost everyone expected, the president ordered me to head west, toward Rome and the Vatican. This was not a surprise to me. Just prior to our departure from Washington, the president had called me aside to tell me that he was seriously thinking of flying from Vietnam to Rome so that he could visit the pope just before Christmas. He instructed me to keep this information in the strictest confidence but that I should take whatever steps were necessary so that he could make that secret stop if he decided to. While still in Washington, I had made arrangements for two presidential helicopters to be dismantled and flown to Spain so that the president could have transportation from the Rome airport to the Vatican.

Now, as we departed Vietnam, our itinerary included a refueling stop in Karachi, where a huge crowd at the airport welcomed LBJ, and he had a short mini-summit with Pakistani President Ayub Khan. Airborne again within an hour, we proceeded across Iran, Turkey, and the Mediterranean Sea, landing in Rome just before midnight on December 23. There, bad news awaited me. I was informed that the two presidential helicopters were still in Spain; although reassembled, they had not yet been test flown, which is required of all presidential aircraft. I said that flying from Spain to Rome would certainly qualify as test-flying and that they should take off immediately. However, we were still left without transportation for the president.

Marvin Watson, the president's chief aide, and I spotted two old American World War II helicopters parked at the airport. We immediately informed the base commander that we were commandeering them for the president. The officer objected that we could not do that, but Watson and I, speaking on behalf of the president, overruled him. We used the old choppers to ferry the presidential party to a retreat where he met representatives of the Italian government. By the time the president was ready to fly from the retreat to the Vatican, the presidential helicopters had arrived, and we used them for the remainder of his short stay, just under four hours, in Italy.

We left Rome for Washington around 2 A.M. by way of a necessary refueling stop in Azores Islands. Shortly after reaching cruising altitude, the president stepped into the cockpit, tapped me on the shoulder, and asked if I had done my Christmas shopping. When I replied in the negative, he then asked if U.S. military forces had a presence and a base exchange (PX) where we were going to land for fuel. I assured him that there was.

He then told me that neither he nor his entourage had accomplished any Christmas shopping either and asked me to call ahead and see if the base commander would open the PX for our arrival. Of course, the commander agreed to do that. Soon after we landed, the local ground crew drove a rather austere school bus up to the exit stair. The president, his guests, my staff, and the entire flight crew boarded it and were driven to the exchange to shop for a couple of hours in the wee hours of the morning of Christmas Eve. A remote Atlantic island and a U.S. Air Force Base with a few of its sleepless people had been treated to a once-in-a-lifetime experience by the thirty-sixth president of the United States.

The journey ended at 7:30 A.M. on Christmas Eve at Andrews AFB, Maryland. One hundred eighteen hours' elapsed time since leaving Washington, this around-the-world flight had consumed fifty-nine hours, thirty minutes' flying time. For the first time in history and perhaps the last, an incumbent president had made a dramatic jet-plane circuit of the globe in less than five days. Such an epic undertaking will likely stand as a record in presidential travels.

Finally, I should add as a postscript that oversight responsibility for maintaining written funeral plans for living former presidents, as well as the incumbent president, was shared by the Military Office in the White House and the Washington Military District commander. It was therefore my responsibility as head of the Military Office to keep President Johnson apprised of such plans. Accordingly, both during his term in office and frequently after his retirement, he would remind me of his mortality and sometimes stop at the family cemetery on his ranch with me in tow. He would point to the spot where one day he would lie in repose, admonish me to keep the plan current, and instruct me to consult often with Mrs. Johnson and their daughters as to their wishes in the matter. That dreaded day came in 1973 when I had the sad duty—which was also a supreme honor and privilege—to assist Mrs. Johnson and the girls through their ordeal during the state funeral. Then, as my last official act on his behalf, I presented Mrs. Johnson his flag, to which my late friend and benefactor had for so long dedicated his soul and his life. The nation had said a tearful good-bye to a visionary and compassionate giant, an uncommon common man.

# Lyndon Johnson: An Awesome Engine of a Man
## Jack Valenti

From my earliest reading, I have always been fascinated with the figure of Achilles. He was so immensely human, a man preeminently noble but led by an excess of his own high nature to flawed action. As the central character in the *Iliad*, he dominates the story even when he is offstage. It is in his sentience, his courage and his anger, his skill, his pride, his commanding presence that of all literary and mythical creations Achilles stands forth as one of the great captains of mortal history.

So it is that I am persuaded that there was much of Achilles in Lyndon Johnson. Indeed, when I wrote a book about him, I wanted to call it *Achilles in the White House*, but my publishers demurred, insisting that orthopedic surgeons might be the only ones to buy the volume.

There will be a considerable body of literature in many books on the Johnson presidency. Not one of them, no matter how strenuous their attempts, will really be definitive on the work President Johnson performed, the deeds he accomplished, the flaws he exhibited, or offer an accurate and total measure of the man himself. To the press that examined his actions and to the public that benefited from his achievements, part of the fascination of Lyndon Johnson is due to the complexity of the man.

I am bound to say that I personally will never look upon his like again in my lifetime, for he cannot be duplicated. He was the largest, most

indomitable political leader I have known or will know. He was an awe-
some engine of a man—terrorizing, tender, inexhaustibly energetic, and
ruthless; loving of land, grass, and water; engulfing, patient, impatient,
caring, and insightful; devoted to wife, family, and friends; petty, clair-
voyant, and compassionate; bullying, sensitive, tough, and resolute;
charming, earthy, courageous, and devious; full of humor, brilliantly intelligent; brutal, wise, suspicious, disciplined, crafty, and generous; and
most of all, possessed of what Mr. Churchill called "the seeing eye . . . the
ability to see beneath the surface of things." He was all of these and more.
He had one goal—to be the greatest president doing the greatest good in
the history of the nation. He had one tragedy—a war the commitments
of which he could not break and the tenacity of which he could not overcome.

I think I knew him as well as anyone beyond his wife and family, and I
know I did not know the full man. Other than Lady Bird Johnson, I daresay no one does.

I admired him greatly and never once wavered in my loyalty to him as
a man and leader. But I never reckoned loyalty and love as barriers to the
perception of faults and flaws. No man or woman is without them. Had
President Johnson been so, he would not borne the barest resemblance to
the towering, endlessly mesmerizing figure he surely was.

Having spent a working lifetime in and around the political arena, as
campaign manager, political counselor and consultant, and as White
House assistant, I have no grand ideas about political leaders. I have
learned that in politics the very best of us is apt to be partly right and
partly wrong. All public men are flawed, inclined toward error, subject to
the vagaries of emotion, afflicted with pride and the infatuation with self
that all of us, public and nonpublic, learn to live with. There are no in-
fallible heroes, bleached dry of sin, unblemished by lesser notions, with
ideals fully intact, and consciences insulated from the need for contrition.

Thus, when we understand that human beings are our leaders, we can
view them with tolerance and forbearance. What we can hope for are
leaders who will be right more often than they are wrong, and we can in-
spire within ourselves expectations no larger than mortal men are capable of delivering. Perhaps we can be forgiven if we ask them to be wiser
than those who give them power; to be possessed of character, vision, and
caring in such dimensions that the tasks they must fulfill will not go un-
served by all their skills and all their courage; and to bring honor to the

duties they have obligated themselves to perform. It is because the public political person is so intensely human that he gives off sparks.

I have worked in two of life's classic fascinations, politics and movies, and while there are dazzling attractions in both areas, it is the political man who most excites me. LBJ was the quintessential political being, and I suppose that is why I was in thrall continuously to him. I was never bored by him or with him; I was either in a stew or a passion.

If in my life now I find it difficult to criticize caustically presidents who followed and will follow Lyndon, it is because I understand so vividly the difficulties that besiege whoever is president. To criticize, the old cliché goes, is easy. To think, to decide, and then to act is terribly hard. To put it in the words of President Johnson—"Any damn jackass can kick a barn down, but it takes a pretty good carpenter to build one."

My knowledge of Lyndon Johnson spans almost the last twenty years of his life, from 1955 until that awful day in January 1973 when he gasped for air in his ranch bedroom and collapsed on the floor, the life gone forever from his human form. I was there in the motorcade on November 22, 1963, when a gallant young president was slain in the streets of Dallas. Within the hour, the new president ordered me aboard Air Force One, hiring me that very moment as special assistant. I flew back to Washington with him. I watched him carefully. While the rest of us were grazing the outer edge of hysteria, unable to confront a nightmarish day with an embrace about as awful as human misery can devise, Lyndon Johnson was calm, thoughtful, steady. LBJ, perhaps the most experienced of all men who have assumed the presidency since the days of our Founding Fathers, remained serene and calm—eerily so. It was as if he put under stern harness all his volcanic passions, resolving to display to the nation that the new leader, confident and assured, was ready to lead his country and the free world. It was a mode I came to know and understand. When the dagger was at the nation's belly, LBJ was cool, undisturbed, clear headed, compassionate of others, ready to face down whatever confrontation had arisen. When the day was empty of crisis, he could be surly, impatient, and sometimes hugely rude. But then, I have already noted that he was massively complicated.

He made two decisions that never-to-be-forgotten day in Dallas. First, though others in Washington urged him otherwise, he determined that Air Force One would not take off without the coffin carrying the thirty-fifth president on board. It was so very wise. Had he left swiftly, leaving the lifeless body of JFK in Dallas, there would have been mutterings indicting him for being too delighted to be president. The second decision was even more prescient. Bobby Kennedy, the attorney general, and others recommended that he get into the air without being sworn in, since constitutionally he was already president. But he said no. He called for Judge Sarah T. Hughes to be dispatched to Love Field and administer the oath. Why? Because he wanted a photograph of that ceremony. When he landed at Andrews Air Force Base near Washington, that negative would be developed and flashed around the world so that an anxious, tremulous world public would know, without doubt, that while the light in the White House may flicker, it never, never goes out. So it was that for over twenty-four hours on TV screens on every continent there was the omnipresent photograph of LBJ, right arm upraised to honor his oath, to his right his wife and to his left the grieving figure of Jacqueline Kennedy. That photograph spoke volumes, perhaps relieving the bursting anxiety of billions of people. It informed the world that in America the Constitution was alive, it worked—the president is dead, but the new president has been sworn in, and the nation goes on.

From Andrews, LBJ flew by chopper to the South Lawn of the White House, landing a little after 6 P.M. I was by his side. It was my first visit to one of the few holy places in America. It would be my workplace for almost three years. He did not use the Oval Office yet, not for three days. He operated out of his Executive Office Building vice-presidential office. By 10 P.M. he had beckoned to me and Bill Moyers, and said "Let's go home." By "home" he meant his residence in Spring Valley, a section of Washington, D.C. Most citizens do not know that LBJ and Mrs. Johnson did not move into the living quarters of the president in the mansion until many days after Dallas.

I spent the night in LBJ's home, as did Cliff Carter and Moyers. Indeed, on Air Force One flying back to Washington, when the new president said, "I want you on my staff," I had blurted out, "but I don't have a place to live there." He smiled, and said, "you can live with me until your family arrives." Thus it was that I lived with the Johnsons, first at their private residence and then for a month and a half in the mansion, on the third floor in a tiny one-bedroom suite.

But it was that first night that I began to measure the greatness of Lyndon Johnson. With Carter, Moyers, and me grouped around him, he lay in his massive king-size bed, and the four of us watched television. We watched as commentators inspected this alien cowboy who was now the leader of the free world. As we sat glued to the TV set, the new president began to ruminate aloud about his plans, his objectives, the great goals he was bound to attain.

As I reach back into my memory of that night, it now seems all quite astounding. On that evening, at that time, I confess, I did not realize the incandescent historic significance of where I was and what I was hearing as LBJ spoke quietly to us. Here we were, Cliff, Bill, and I, sitting around a bed in which a huge form of a man sat propped up, eyes and ears fastened on the screen—the same man whom a billion or so people throughout the world were surveying and whom in a hundred different languages presidents, prime ministers, journalists, clerics, philosophers, and historians were taking stock of as the man who had replaced the heroic John Fitzgerald Kennedy.

LBJ, without really expecting us to respond, began to expatiate with relish and resolve. "I'm going to get Kennedy's tax cut out of the Senate Finance Committee, and we're going to get this economy humming again. Then I'm going to pass Kennedy's civil rights bill, which has been hung up too long in the Congress. And I'm going to pass it without changing a single comma or a word. After that we'll pass legislation that allows everyone anywhere in this country to vote, with all the barriers down. And that's not all. We're going to get a law that says every boy and girl in this country, no matter how poor, or the color of their skin, or the region they come from, is going to be able to get all the education they can take by loan, scholarship, or grant, right from the federal government." He stopped speaking for a moment then continued, "and I aim to pass Harry Truman's medical insurance bill that got nowhere before."

Suddenly it was now about 4 A.M. on the morning of November 23. LBJ had been president for some fifteen hours, and he already sketched out what later became known as the Great Society. Within two months, the tax cut was indeed sprung from the Senate and went into overdrive to jump-start the economy. Within two years, the Civil Rights Act of 1964, the Voting Rights Act of 1965, medical insurance legislation better known as Medicare, the Elementary and Secondary Education Act and a dozen more education bills, as well as many more in the areas of conservation, consumer safety, beautification, and the War on Poverty, with its Head Start program and the Job Corps—all were extracted from a sometimes recalcitrant Congress, to the applause of the country.

What Lyndon Johnson did was no less than ignite a political and social revolution, attacking the ills of the land across a broad front, in a relentless, ceaseless advance that ran down antagonist members of Congress and laid siege to old prejudices, breaking the back of resistance and introducing to the nation new obligations too long ignored. He had reigned over the Senate with a ceaseless capacity to govern that ego-driven, disparate assembly. Now he worked his magic in the Oval Office, cajoling, threatening, embracing, persuading, whether on the telephone, in his office, in the State Dining Room, or the East Room. Never before or since, with the possible exception of FDR in the New Deal period and the war years, had a president exerted such power, mustered such persuasion, mastered such opposition, passing literally every piece of legislation that he counted vital. It was astonishing to both friend and foe alike.

Odd it was that there was no mention of Vietnam that first night of his presidency. The president made no reference to the over 16,000 U.S. fighting men deployed to that distant part of the world, a landscape and culture unknown to, and casually regarded by, the great majority of Americans. During that first night none of us, and surely not LBJ, saw a future wherein Vietnam would become a fungus on the face of the Johnson administration, soiling an impossibly large legacy, the greatest political procession ever led by a president (again excepting FDR) before or since, with the mission to raise the quality of life in this land.

A question that no one asks: "If there had been no American soldiers in Vietnam on November 22, 1963, would President Johnson have sent them there?" It is a question that cannot be answered. But I daresay, given the necessity of funding for the Great Society programs, which a war in Asia would surely diminish, and knowing of LBJ's distaste for military adventures in Asia, I personally believe most passionately that he would not have intervened. He was terribly disturbed by the assassination of President Diem of South Vietnam in October 1963, and he privately blamed certain U.S. foreign policy officials for having apparently unleashed discontented Vietnamese generals clamoring for the scalp of Diem. It was a messy, ugly business. LBJ found it unsettling. But we will never know the answer to the question.

Let me tell you a story in which is enfolded the unornamented central character of this large man of large spirit and large vision for America. It was on a Sunday morning in early December 1963. Since I was living on the third floor of the Mansion, I spent considerable time with President Johnson. On this Sunday morning, as I had coffee with him in the West Hall of his private living quarters, he said, "Call Dick Russell. See if he will visit with us and have some coffee." I did as I was bid and later went down to the Diplomatic Reception Room to greet Senator Russell.

Perhaps today not too many will be familiar with Richard Brevard Russell, former governor of Georgia and in 1963 the senior senator from that southern state. He was also the preeminent, most influential member of the Senate. He bestrode the chamber of that body with graceful authority. He was erudite, vastly intelligent, a master of the classics, a man whose word was unbreakable, as every senator knew, and who was inhabited by integrity so rooted in his being that none disputed his prestige. He had one flaw, absent which he could have become president—he was the leader of the segregation forces in the Senate.

When we got to the second floor, Russell, a slight figure, was enthusiastically embraced by the six-foot-four LBJ, obviously delighted that his old friend had arrived. When in 1952 the Senate Democratic leader had been defeated in his home state, the other Senate Democrats urged Russell to become leader. "No," he had said, "Lyndon Johnson should be our leader." At that moment, LBJ was a freshman senator, in the fourth year of his first term. It was unprecedented that a senator so new to his duties would be made leader. But at age forty-four, LBJ became the youngest Democratic leader in the history of the Senate and promptly proved himself the greatest parliamentary commander that that hundred-member body ever had.

The president and Russell sat in the West Hall, Russell in a green couch backed up to a window through which one could see the Rose Garden in all its glory. LBJ sat next to him, in a wing chair, their knees almost touching. I sat next to Russell. The president grabbed Russell by the shoulder, almost a caress, and said softly, "Dick, I asked you here to tell you I am grateful to you. Without you, I would never have become leader, I would never have been vice president, and I certainly wouldn't be here this day. So I love you, and I owe you. Which is why I want to tell you, please don't get in my way on this civil rights bill, which has been blocked too long, because if you do, I'll run you down." The president's voice was quiet and somber.

Russell sat impassively. Then, in that soft accent derived from his Georgia countryside, he said to LBJ, "Well, suh, you may very well do that, but if you do, you will not only lose the election, you will lose the South forever." The words were spoken without antagonism but with resignation that was mirrored in his piercing blue eyes. The president reached forward to touch Russell affectionately on the shoulder. He said in a very low voice, "Well, Dick, if that's the price I have to pay, I will pay it gladly."

In all the future years I knew Lyndon Johnson, I was never prouder of him than that long-ago Sunday morning so early in his presidency. It was for me a blazing illumination of how one defines leadership, the willingness to imperil a personal political future in order to do what is right by the people you have by solemn oath sworn to serve.

How to sum up Lyndon Johnson? If it could be done, one would have to start with the singular essential of the man. LBJ cared about the poor, cared deeply about the humblest in this nation. Lying just beneath the surface of his emotions was a tireless compulsion that may have infected him when he was a young student in college, when during an off-period he taught school in the little town of Cotulla, in south Texas. The school was a run-down, one-room teaching platform, totally populated by Mexican children, the offspring of migrant workers. He was deeply affected by this experience. He struggled with the frustration of knowing that these children were not going to be educated in such a way as to offer them the promise of the American dream. He yearned to make a difference in their lives. Many years later, when he became president, he said, "Now that I have the power, I aim to use it"—meaning that he was now ready to do something about revising radically the imbalance in the lives of those pressed against the wall by circumstances over which they had no control.

This became a passion with LBJ. When he came to the White House he was armed with convictions from which he never swerved and to which was connected almost every piece of legislation he devised. Lord Macaulay once wrote that "a man without convictions will be right only by accident." Conviction is to a great president as oxygen is to life. To such a leader no obstacle is too immense, no moat too wide, no mood too bleak, and no opposition is so firm that he ever considers hesitance or meek compromise—certainly not failure. Conviction is what powers the leader. Without it, not only will success be accidental, but success will be too loosely fibered to last as a legacy.

To "see" Lyndon Johnson, you must understand conviction. Churchill's words embody LBJ's passionate conviction, which was the secret of his legislative triumphs: "Nothing could overcome his central will or rupture his sense of duty."

# Some Aspects of
# Lyndon Johnson's Personality
*Sherwin J. Markman*

Every person who served on Lyndon Johnson's White House staff knows dozens of anecdotes illustrating the multifaceted complexities of the thirty-sixth American president. Here are two of my own.

Ten days after the successful conclusion of the Six Day War between Israel and all the surrounding Arab states, the Soviet premier, Alexis Kosygin, traveled to New York City to attend a session of the United Nations. President Johnson saw this as an opportunity to meet with the Soviet leader and lessen the extraordinary tension that had developed between the two countries because of both the Six Day War and the conflict in Vietnam. Accordingly, the president sent an invitation to Premier Kosygin, stating that inasmuch as Kosygin was visiting in the United States, he would be most welcome at the White House.

Kosygin replied that he would be delighted to see the president. However, Kosygin added, he did not consider his appearance at the United Nations to be a visit to the United States. He stated that it was not appropriate for him to come to the White House, but he would be happy to see the president at the United Nations in New York City.

President Johnson did not accept Kosygin's reasoning, and for a time it appeared that the two leaders had reached an impasse and that there would be no meeting between them. However, both sides felt that such a result would be ridiculous, and an effort was made to find a compromise. What was finally done was to get a map, take a ruler, lay one end of the ruler on the White House and the other on the United Nations headquarters, and then note the location that was precisely halfway between the two points. That place was Glassboro, New Jersey, the home of an institution then called Glassboro State Teachers College.

The agreement that was reached at five o'clock in the afternoon called for the two leaders to meet at Glassboro at eleven o'clock the following morning, June 23, 1967. At six o'clock, a public announcement was made.

Shortly before seven o'clock, Marvin Watson, the president's chief of staff, called me and told me to come to his office immediately. My own office was on the second floor of the West Wing, and his adjoined the president's Oval Office. I scurried down the stairs and burst in on Marvin, who, as usual, was busily handling telephone calls with the assistance of his marvelous secretary, Mary Jo Cook, with whom he shared his cramped quarters.

Marvin informed me that I would be heading a team of people going to Glassboro to prepare for a summit conference the next day between the president and Kosygin, and that he expected the group to assemble and be ready to depart from Andrews Air Force Base in one hour. The group I was to lead would include Secret Service agents, military members of the White House communications office, people from the White House press office, Richard Moose from the National Security Council staff, plus navy personnel who were in charge of the White House mess. Marvin had already alerted all of them, and they would, he told me, assemble on time at Andrews.

Marvin went on to tell me that although the campus of Glassboro State Teachers College had been agreed upon as the site of the summit, the college's officials had not yet been officially informed. I would have to do that, obtain their permission, and with them decide upon and prepare the precise location for the conference. I would also have to coordinate my activities with the New Jersey state officials detailed by its governor, Richard Hughes, who had already been alerted and would be meeting me upon my arrival. Marvin emphasized that I would have to be diplomatic with both the officials and the people from the college, and take great care not to upset anyone. Nonetheless, subject to his and the president's approval, I should never forget that I was in charge.

"The president has several quite specific requirements he wants you to arrange at whatever place the meeting takes place," Marvin continued. "There should be rugs on the floor so that when aides walk around there will be no noise. There must be a room for a conference large enough so that up to twenty people can comfortably sit, but it should be sufficiently informal so that there is an atmosphere of intimacy. The chairs should be comfortable, and the president wants a large, padded rocking chair for himself. It is also important that this conference room should adjoin another large room where the aides to the president and Kosygin can separately meet. Finally, there must be a third room, one very intimately furnished, where the president, Kosygin, and their interpreters can privately meet, if they so desire."

When I arrived at Andrews, not everyone on the team had yet arrived, and understandably there was a delay before everyone was assembled and ready to depart. It was past nine o'clock before we were airborne on the small presidential Lockheed Jetstar, headed for Philadelphia, the closest airport to Glassboro. We landed at ten o'clock at night.

Our White House team was met on the tarmac by a motorcade of New Jersey state police, who convoyed us on the hour's drive to Glassboro. It was close to 11 P.M. when we drove up to the front entrance of the large Victorian residence of Dr. Thomas Robinson, the president of the college. Accompanied by the state police chief, I walked up to the door of the mansion, which I later learned was named "Hollybush." We had to push our way through a throng of reporters who had already assembled and had been waiting for us.

I knocked on the door and introduced myself to Dr. Robinson and his wife, who, of course, knew why we had come. By then, we had less than twelve hours to pull it all together.

Dr. Robinson was cordial and wanted to be as helpful as possible, but Mrs. Robinson was nervous and apprehensive. Dr. Robinson told me that he had been thinking of where on the small campus the meetings should be held. He told me that his recommendation was the auditorium in the college administration building, and he asked us to follow him there. At this point, Governor Hughes arrived and joined our group as we walked across the campus.

As soon as we stepped inside the auditorium, I realized that this facility would not work. It was far too sterile. As politely as possible, I told Dr. Robinson that we must find another location. Actually, I had already decided that the only place that came close to meeting the president's requirements was Hollybush, the large residence of Dr. and Mrs. Robinson.

As soon as we returned to Hollybush, I told the Robinsons that their home would suit us perfectly. Then, with Mrs. Robinson's grudging consent, the entire group carefully explored the old house. It had a large living room (for meetings of the full delegations from both nations), Dr. Robinson's small study (for any private session between the president and Kosygin), a spacious kitchen, and a big formal dining room. It clearly would do.

However, there were a few problems, all of which had to be solved that night. The first obstacle was a total lack of air conditioning. It was already a warm June night, and the forecast for the next day called for hot and humid weather. Hollybush was over one hundred years old. Not only did it have no cooling, but its wiring would not support the power necessary for operating even minimal window units. Worse yet, the power coming into the house was inadequate unless the electrical company furnished a new outside transformer

These and other problems were dealt with through the long night. The power company delivered and installed an outdoor transformer, electricians rewired the house, fourteen window air-conditioning units were located and connected, and before dawn the old house could be made comfortably cool.

A plethora of other problems also confronted us. Among them was the necessity of obtaining a large conference table and chairs, finding and installing heavy-duty kitchen equipment to prepare a formal luncheon, constructing and installing doors between the meeting rooms, placing heavy drapes over the windows to ensure privacy, installing private telephones for the Soviet and American delegations, and constructing a security fence that would keep the press and public a safe distance from the conferees. In addition, much of the Robinsons' furniture had to be removed to make room for the meeting. To accomplish all this, over fifty people with a great variety of skills were summoned, came, and worked throughout the night. Miraculously, everything was completed on time.

As the night wore on, Mrs. Robinson became increasingly distraught about what was being done to her home. From time to time, I had to stop all the workmen while I did my best to calm her. At 3 A.M., I finally persuaded her to try to get some sleep, but before dawn she was back, more nervous than ever.

At around 7 A.M., I reported to Marvin that all would be ready, and I dictated a scenario for the president that contained my suggestions concerning the day's meetings and luncheon, now only five hours away. An hour later, Marvin told me that the president had approved my report. Basically, it called for the president to arrive in Glassboro by helicopter at 11 A.M., five minutes before Kosygin's motorcade would get there from New York City. The president would greet Kosygin at the front entrance of Hollybush. The two delegations would then meet for two hours, break for lunch together, and conclude their day with more meetings until their adjournment, which was scheduled for 3 P.M. At that time, Kosygin would drive back to New York, and the president would helicopter to the Philadelphia airport, where Air Force One would be waiting to fly him to Los Angeles to attend a large fund-raising dinner.

While the president, along with Mrs. Johnson and Marvin, were flying to Glassboro, one of the FBI agents who had been delegated to be present at the summit conference approached me and asked to be shown the private room that had been set aside for meetings of the Soviet delegation. That room was located on the second floor of Hollybush, and I stood by while the agent carefully examined it.

"If it's all right with you, we would like to secretly plant some microphones around this room," the agent told me.

I was startled, and after thinking for a moment, shook my head, and said, "I don't think that you should do that."

"Why not?" the agent asked. "This is a golden opportunity to gather intelligence. We shouldn't waste it."

"The risk is too great," I answered. "If they find out that we tried bugging them here, that might blow everything apart."

"I guarantee they won't discover anything," the agent said.

"I won't argue that, but I don't want to take a chance. Since the president is airborne right now and there's no one at the White House I can check with, I'll have to make this decision on my own."

The agent did not press me further. However, when I told Marvin about it later, he shrugged, and said, "What the FBI probably did was install the listening devices with or without your consent. That's the way they operate. If they really thought it was an important intelligence opportunity, you can bet they didn't waste it just because you didn't like it."

A short time later, I watched as the presidential helicopter landed on the college baseball field. The president, with Mrs. Johnson and Marvin at his side, strode toward me. "All right, tell me what you have planned for me," the president barked. I started to explain the schedule that the president himself had approved earlier that morning—a schedule that was to begin almost immediately, because Kosygin's motorcade from New York was due to arrive at any moment. But the president interrupted my recitation and growled, "I don't like it!"

I began to stutter a reply to the effect that there was no time left to change anything, but at that moment Mrs. Johnson stepped between the president and me. Turning to face her husband, she quietly stated in her lovely, lilting South Texas drawl, "Now, Lyndon, please try to understand that Sherwin has worked all night on this. I am certain that he has done an excellent job, and I think you should do it his way." The president flushed, but after a moment's hesitation, he shrugged and said to me, "All right, let's get going."

Later, I told Mrs. Johnson that I would be forever grateful to her for that moment of intervention. Right then was no time to make a single change in the plans. Quite literally, Kosygin and his people were entering Glassboro.

The president greeted the premier as his car drove up to Hollybush. After some preliminary photographs, the meetings between the two delegations began. A few minutes later, the president asked Kosygin if he would like to meet privately. Kosygin immediately agreed, and the two leaders, accompanied only by their translators and Marvin Watson, went into Dr. Robinson's adjoining study for a private meeting.

A few days later, when the president saw his daughter, Luci, and (for the first time) his newborn grandson, Lyndon, he would tell her how he had used the fact of Lyndon's birth to emphasize the opportunities for peace that he and the premier shared. Luci remembers her father saying that he had told Kosygin, "My younger daughter, Luci, is just giving birth to my first grandchild. I know that you too are a grandfather, and I have been thinking that you and I are only two of millions of grandfathers around the world, but there is an immense difference between all the others and us. We can actually accomplish something that will make the world a safer place for our grandchildren. That is our great blessing as well as our responsibility." Luci has since said that she has never forgotten how touched she was by her father's use of her son's birth in the cause of peace.

At the luncheon for the senior members of both delegations, Secretary of Defense Robert S. McNamara, seated two chairs away from Premier Kosygin, leaned past the president, who was between them, and with far more emotion than I had ever heard from him expressed his vision of the tragedy that would follow a nuclear holocaust. McNamara emphasized how the entire world would suffer immense destruction and loss of life and that such a horror must, at any cost, be avoided. Kosygin listened impassively to McNamara's plea before dryly remarking that, most assuredly, he shared McNamara's concern.

While the leaders of the two superpowers were enjoying their sumptuous lunch at Hollybush, I led the small group of Kosygin's Kremlin aides to the college cafeteria for a quick bite to eat. The menu there was hot dogs and baked beans. I was embarrassed and apologetic when the Russians pulled out several tins of caviar and insisted that we all share their expensive delicacy. They also produced a bottle of vodka, which, with some reluctance, we refused. It was a relaxed, pleasant lunch, during which we exchanged anecdotes concerning our surprisingly similar problems of working for powerful bosses. However, when the issue of Vietnam was broached the conversation became tense, and the subject quickly was changed.

As the two leaders concluded their private meeting, they discussed whether it made sense for them to meet again before Kosygin returned to Moscow. They agreed that their meeting had gone reasonably well and should be continued. However, the Soviets had to return to New York City, and the president was scheduled to fly to Los Angeles that evening. Nonetheless, they decided to return to Glassboro on Sunday, two days later.

On the flight to Los Angeles, the president told Marvin that he would like to obtain the two chairs and the small table in Dr. Robinson's study that he and Kosygin had used for their private meetings. The president said that the furniture would make an interesting display at the presidential library he already was considering.

Marvin called me from Air Force One and instructed me to arrange to purchase that furniture from Dr. and Mrs. Robinson. When I returned to Glassboro on Saturday morning to prepare for the Sunday summit meeting, I sat down with the Robinsons and relayed the president's wishes to them. I explained that their furniture would become a historical artifact for which the government would pay them a fair price.

"You can have the little table and one of the chairs," Mrs. Robinson said. "But the rocking chair has been a family heirloom for generations and I don't want to part with it."

"What if we have the best craftsman we can find make an exact duplicate of that chair and give it to you?" I asked.

"Then you use the duplicate at the president's library," Mrs. Robinson snapped.

It was apparent that Mrs. Robinson was quite upset, and I did not pursue the subject further. Instead, I called Marvin and passed on Mrs. Robinson's suggestion that the duplicate be used at the president's library. Marvin put the idea to the president, who immediately rejected it and told Marvin to instruct me to get the job done.

It was obvious that I needed help with Mrs. Robinson, so I contacted Governor Hughes, explained the problem, and asked him to persuade her to part with her rocking chair. The governor immediately called the Robinsons. A short while later, when I again sat down with Mrs. Robinson, she told me that she had changed her mind after listening to the governor and that she would be honored to see her furniture displayed at the Johnson Library. And that is where the two chairs and the little table can now be seen, enshrined within a glass case honoring the Glassboro summit conference.

As planned, on Sunday both delegations returned to Glassboro to resume their meetings. This time, however, Premier Kosygin brought his daughter with him. When we learned that she planned to attend, we hastily arranged for Mrs. Johnson to return to Glassboro along with the Johnsons' older daughter, Lynda. The president's helicopter took the ladies on a leisurely flight over the more scenic parts of New Jersey while the afternoon conference was taking place. Mrs. Johnson, as always, was a gracious hostess during their excursion, but she later said that Kosygin's daughter was nervous and kept asking when they would return, because her father was insistent that they should never be tardy.

It was late Sunday afternoon when the conference adjourned. As we were saying our good-byes, we learned that Premier Kosygin had scheduled an 8 P.M. televised press conference to be held at the United Nations. President Johnson immediately decided that he also should appear on television to report on the summit conference but that his report should be made prior to Kosygin's. By that time, we were on the helicopter bound for Philadelphia, where Air Force One awaited us. Once on board, the pilot, Colonel James

Cross, told the president that if Air Force One were to land, as it normally did, at Andrews Air Force Base, there was no way that the president could be transported to the White House before the Kosygin press conference.

The president asked Colonel Cross if there was anything that could be done to speed things up. "Well, sir, we could land Air Force One at National Airport," Colonel Cross suggested. "That would save just enough time to get you to the White House and on television before Kosygin. There is just one problem. Landing this big airplane at National would violate one or two FAA regulations. Planes our size are not permitted in and out of that airport. The runway is considered too short."

"But can you land us safely?" the president asked.

"Yes, sir, I can."

"Then do it," the president ordered.

Because he was piloting Air Force One, the control tower at National gave Colonel Cross clearance to land there. We touched down smoothly, and all of us scurried to the helicopter waiting to whisk us to the White House. As I hurried behind the president, I noticed that the front wheels of Air Force One had come to a stop only a few feet short of the end of the runway. I was happy not to have known that in advance. The president, on the other hand, was pleased that he was able to get on television before Kosygin.

In early November 1967, the president decided that he would take a weekend off and travel with his family to historic Williamsburg, Virginia, for two days of worry-free relaxation away from the pressures of the war, the screaming antiwar protestors, and his indecision as whether or not he should seek reelection. What he wanted to do was attend the festive annual Gridiron Dinner on Saturday evening (which was always an enjoyable and humorous occasion for him) and then attend church on Sunday, followed by a round of golf with his daughter's fiancé, Marine captain Charles Robb. It was a fine idea, and he asked me to travel to Williamsburg to prepare the way for him.

"Just make damn certain that whatever church you choose for me doesn't have some publicity-hungry minister who will take advantage of my presence," the president instructed. "I don't want him sermonizing me on any political matters."

I assured the president that I would be careful.

On Friday, November 10, together with several Secret Service agents, I drove to Williamsburg. Finding a lovely home for the First Family proved to be no problem. Historic Williamsburg was owned by the Rockefeller family, and its representative on that subject was Arkansas governor Lawrence Rockefeller. I spoke to the governor, and he made Bassett House available. The home was perfect, a large colonial mansion, with floorboards dating back to before the Revolutionary War; it was exquisitely situated within spacious, tree-lined grounds. The governor also made arrangements for the president and his guests to play golf on Sunday at the Williamsburg golf course. The final item I broached with the governor was the subject of church for the president and his family on Sunday.

The governor's response was immediate. "There is no question but that the president should attend the most historic church in Williamsburg, Bruton Parish Episcopal."

"Who is the minister there?" I asked.

"Cotesworth Lewis," the governor responded. "I've known him for years. He's a good man."

"Is there any chance he might say anything that might embarrass the president?" I asked.

"Absolutely none," the governor said. "He thinks highly of President Johnson. I'm sure of that."

"Would you talk to him anyway?" I asked. "We need to be sure."

"I'm happy to do that," the governor said. "If there's any problem, I'll let you know immediately. If you don't hear from me, everything is fine."

I never heard from the governor, and thus I assumed that the governor had a satisfactory conversation with Reverend Lewis. Nonetheless, knowing how strongly the president felt on the subject of being trapped in the congregation of a haranguing minister, I decided to visit with Reverend Lewis personally.

I was somewhat worried that the minister might accuse me of attempting to "censor" him, if the man decided to play that game, so I first spoke with the Secret Service agent in charge of ensuring security for the president in Williamsburg. I suggested to the agent, "If the president is planning to attend the Bruton Parish Church, isn't it appropriate for you to check out the minister to make sure that neither he nor anyone else there will be a threat while the president attends his church?"

"Of course," the agent agreed.

The two of us called on Reverend Lewis that afternoon. Lewis, a courtly and impressively earnest man, was relaxed and friendly when we sat with him in the small study of his church.

"I hope that you understand the reason for my questions," I began. "The president is considering attending your church tomorrow morning. If that causes you any difficulty, just tell us now and we will have him go elsewhere."

"No, not at all," Reverend Lewis replied. "I will be honored to have him seated as our honored guest."

I probed further, frankly raising the subject most on my mind. "What about your sermon, sir? We need to be certain that you will not take advantage of the president's presence to embarrass him"

Smiling broadly, Reverend Lewis shook his head, apparently taking no offense at my questions. "I would never do anything like that," he stated. Then, without being asked, he handed the Secret Service agent and me several typed pages. "This is the sermon I will give tomorrow," he said. "You can see there is nothing in it that will bother the president."

The agent and I quickly read the document. It contained nothing political. I was relieved and satisfied and I returned the sermon to Lewis. "All of us appreciate your willingness to cooperate," I told him.

"It will be a proud moment for me, and an historic occasion for our church," Lewis said.

A short while later, I called Marvin and gave him a full report on what I had done. I told him that the Secret Service, Governor Rockefeller, and I were all satisfied that the president had no cause for concern with Reverend Lewis. I added that the president could look forward to a carefree weekend.

On Saturday evening, I spent the most relaxing time I was ever to share with President Johnson. Following the Gridiron Dinner, after everyone else in his family had gone to bed, the president was sitting alone and sipping a scotch in the living room of the loaned Rockefeller house in Williamsburg. I was standing in the hallway making some final preparations when he motioned to me and asked me to come in and join him for a drink.

The president was all smiles as he pointed toward the bar and told me to fix myself whatever I wanted. Then the two of us sat together and chatted. The president was contented and happy, regaling me with anecdotes and hilariously repeating some of the Gridiron skits that had amused him at the dinner. Finally, the president, his arm draped around me, walked me to the door and said goodnight. "You are a fine young man," he said. "I am so proud that you are serving on my staff." I felt like I was floating on a cloud.

That evening with the president was the highpoint of my years at the White House. I felt that, for the first time, I had truly glimpsed the heart of Lyndon Johnson. I went to bed basking in the good feelings I had experienced. Unfortunately, the next day was destined to be the beginning of the worst week I was ever to experience.

Sunday began innocently enough, when I joined the president and his family as their motorcade drove the short distance to the Bruton Parish Church. I did not accompany them inside the church, because there were a few remaining details that needed to be handled. However, along with several Secret Service agents and a large group of reporters, I watched as the First Family entered the church.

About an hour later, I was standing among the crowd outside the church who were waiting for the president to emerge from the service. Suddenly, the door to the church burst open, and the pool reporters ran out, shouting to their colleagues, "You'll never believed what just happened in there!"

For an instant I had a vision of a shooting or a heart attack, but then I overheard one of the pool reporters yell, "That reverend just gave the president holy hell!"

I did not need to hear another word. I felt like I was going to throw up, and I quickly walked to the end of the waiting presidential motorcade and stood behind the last car, trying to be as inconspicuous as possible, wishing that I could disappear. At that moment, the president and Mrs. Johnson came out of the church, both of them displaying tight smiles. The president stood on the top step, and I saw the president's head slowly turn as his eyes swept over the waiting crowd. I had no doubt what the president was doing, and my worst fear was confirmed when the president's gaze finally located me. Then, his eyes glaring, the president motioned to me to come join him. Taking a deep breath, I walked toward the president, wishing that I could be anywhere else in the world but right there.

"Go sit in my car," the president snapped at me.

I did as I was told, dreading what I knew was coming.

In the presidential limousine, the president told me what had happened during the church service. He said that he and his family, trapped in their pew, had been subjected to a vicious verbal assault by the "trustworthy" Reverend Cotesworth Pinckney Lewis. In short, everything that I had tried to avoid had come to pass.

In an ominously quiet voice, he told me that all had gone normally during the formal portion of the Episcopal service; the president and Mrs.

Johnson, together with their daughter Lynda and Chuck Robb, had been enjoying the occasion, especially the marvelous church choir; and then, out of the blue, Reverend Lewis walked to the pulpit, began his sermon, and everything changed.

As the president related the incident to me, I was shocked that Lewis had deliberately lied to the Secret Service and me about the sermon he planned to give while the president sat before him. The so-called draft sermon he had handed to us had been a total falsity. Lewis's perfidy would be made even clearer by his actions immediately following the church service. He stood outside his church distributing to the press mimeographed copies of his actual sermon, in an effort to take full advantage of his few moments of fame.

Lewis had spent his entire time excoriating the president regarding American actions in Vietnam. Lewis had accused the president of furnishing American troops with "inadequate" equipment and inhibiting them with his "confusing" directions. It had been a horribly painful experience for the president and his family. The president said that he had been tempted to stand and defend himself against the unprovoked attack, but he had exercised self-control, knowing that anything he said or did would only make matters worse. So, helplessly, he bore the brunt of the Reverend's deliberately planned attack upon him.

When the president arrived back at the Rockefeller house, all of his pent-up anger and frustration exploded, and since he could do nothing to Reverend Lewis, his full wrath was directed at me. "How in the hell could you have let that happen?" the president shouted at me. "Didn't I warn you? Weren't you listening to me?"

I tried to explain all that I had done, but the president would not listen. His ranting at me continued without letup. When I managed to sputter that Lewis had lied to me, the president was not mollified. "You are supposed to be a smart boy," the president growled. "You should have seen through him. That son of a bitch took you in, and the Secret Service too. None of you are worth a damn to me!"

When Mrs. Johnson slipped into the room and gently reminded the president that he was scheduled to play golf with Chuck Robb, the president nodded and followed Mrs. Johnson out of the room. Briefly, I had the hope that the president's harangue was over, but it disappeared when he turned back toward me, and stated, "I'm not finished with you. Stay right here until I get back."

I did as I was told. For several hours, I sat alone in the Rockefeller living room, skipping lunch as I anxiously waited. Above all else, I wanted out. I knew that there was nothing I could have done to avoid the deliberate scheme of a determined preacher willing to lie in order to achieve his goal. But the president believed otherwise, so much so that I was convinced that I was about to be fired or forced to resign. If I could have done so, at that moment I would have quit and run away. But I sat there and waited.

I had a faint hope that the round of golf somehow would calm the president, but that disappeared the moment the scowling president strode back into the room. Then, as if he had never stopped, the president continued to berate me. It was awful.

I assumed that the ordeal finally would end when the president departed to board the helicopter for the short flight back to the White House while I returned in one of the Secret Service automobiles. But when that time came, my hope for a reprieve was shattered; the president ordered me to get on the helicopter with him.

Throughout that noisy journey from Williamsburg to Washington, the president continued his attack on me. I was embarrassed and distressed, as were Mrs. Johnson and the rest of the group on the helicopter, but the president's anger was incendiary, and no one tried to interfere. By now, I had ceased all efforts to defend myself, and doing my hopeless best to meet the president's angry gaze, I merely sat and absorbed every shouted word hurled at me.

Even after we landed on the South Lawn of the While House, the ordeal continued. Instead of releasing me to go home, the president directed me to accompany him into the mansion. There, in the Yellow Sitting Room on the second floor, I was forced to bear another half hour of the president's wrath. Finally, the president told me that I was free to go home, and I spoke up.

"I will resign in the morning, Mr. President," I said.

"Like hell you will!" the president shot back. "You're not quitting until I say you can!"

I was puzzled, but so beaten down that I did not argue. I simply nodded my head as I departed.

The following morning, feeling thoroughly defeated, I was waiting in Marvin's office when he returned from the daily meeting with the president in his bedroom. Marvin told me that the president was still angry about his experience on Sunday. He told me that he had attempted to calm the president—and to defend me—but it was hopeless. The president had not listened to Marvin, who had merely dropped the subject.

Now, alone with Marvin in his office, I repeated everything I had done trying to forestall an attack on the president in Williamsburg. Watson told me that he was convinced that nothing more could have been done, and that, eventually, the president would understand.

"But the president won't listen to me," I plaintively said. "If he feels that way, then I should quit."

"Don't!" Marvin stated. "The president will calm down. I'm sure of it. I know he likes you. Just give him a little time."

"I can't take much more, Marvin."

"Just suck it up," Watson said. "It's going to pass."

Sadly, I nodded my head.

"I have a suggestion," Watson said. "Since he won't listen to you—or me either, for that matter—why don't you write him a memo detailing everything you did. I'll make sure he reads it. Maybe it will make a difference."

Feeling hopeless, I nonetheless wrote my report, and a couple of hours later I handed it to Marvin. That evening Marvin included it among the president's night reading. The next morning, when the president handed back the stack of papers, Watson saw that the president had initialed my memo without comment, but the president said nothing to him about it.

The president never again mentioned the subject to me, and I was never fired.

Several weeks later, I was invited to attend a formal White House dinner honoring a foreign dignitary. When I walked through the receiving line, the broadly smiling president gripped my elbow, squeezing it gently. Then, turning to the guest of honor, the president said, "I want you to meet one of my most trusted assistants and one of the brightest young men I know." Realizing that at last the president's anger had passed, I basked in the glow of what I knew was presidential over-praise intended to make up, somehow, for the hell through which both of us had suffered.

SECTION THREE

# Measure Each Word:
# Johnson the Communicator

Johnson insiders have long noted that LBJ was not merely interested in mass media but obsessed by it. In particular, he appears to have had an excessive concern with his personal image, both aural and visual. Jack McNulty examines the manner in which the president attempted to control that image and communicate his message to the American people; he raises many interesting questions for future scholars about the former president's ability to convey his vision. Did Johnson have personal problems with his image because of unfair comparisons with his predecessor, John Kennedy? What were Johnson's strengths and weaknesses as a communicator? Why was Johnson so charismatic, persuasive, and effective as a communicator one on one or with small groups but unable to transfer that ability to national public audiences? Does style today count for more than substance in national political figures?

# Words Mattered:
# Johnson the Communicator
## *Jack McNulty*

"Can you all count to four?" President Lyndon Johnson in 1966 was lecturing his speechwriters about brevity. Now you've all been to college. Four. That's what I want you to remember. Can you do that?" The teacher who once taught poor Mexican children in Cotulla, Texas, leaned forward and flipped up the fingers on his huge hand.

"Four. It's like making love to a woman. If you don't get your idea across in the first four minutes, you won't do it. Four sentences to a paragraph. Four letters to a word. The most important words in the English language all have four letters. Home. Love. Food. Land. Peace. I know, "peace" has five letters, but any damn fool knows it should have four."

President Johnson cared about speeches, and words mattered. Like every politician of his day, he saw speeches as a principal way of communicating to the people. Unlike a press conference or an interview, a speech gave the initiative to the speaker. He could choose the topic and the time, set the tone, organize the thoughts, show the conviction of his beliefs and the fire of his personality. Well written and well delivered, a speech could convince and persuade its listeners. Or by God, it ought to.

For a president, public speaking is only one available means. He can send messages to Congress, hold press conferences, give interviews, issue proclamations and executive orders, write letters to prominent individuals.

To Lyndon Johnson, all were important: they conveyed ideas and could change minds. He wanted all his public papers to contain something quotable, a sentence or paragraph that would be appear in the next day's newspaper. Words had power; words mattered.

Lyndon Johnson was no recluse. Outgoing, friendly, larger than life, he loved being with and talking to people. Shaking hands at an airport, meeting with congressmen, speaking before audiences large or small, using the telephone as a tool of conversation and persuasion, and even walking the White House fence to visit with the tourists. Sadly, in the latter days of his presidency, such impromptu excursions became more infrequent, as friendly tourists became mixed with demonstrators opposed to the Vietnam War.

All who knew LBJ as candidate and congressman saw him as a rousing, forceful, and arresting speaker. He had a Texan's gift for anecdote and a voice that could carry to the farthest reaches of a crowd. In a smaller setting, he would modulate his voice almost to a murmur. His listeners would bend forward. Then he would raise his voice to a sudden shout and hammer home his point with repetition, gestures, and the force of his presence.

He came to the presidency with a far-reaching domestic agenda that he would bring to fruition in the historic programs of the Great Society. He knew what ought and needed to be done in civil rights, in health and education, and in lifting the poor from poverty. A populist from his roots, his driving ambition was to fulfill the ideals of the FDR's New Deal and Truman's Fair Deal. But to do this he had to persuade, cajole, and ultimately convince not only the Congress but all the American people.

By late 1963, television had become the gateway to the American mind. For the politician, it had supplanted radio and the stump speech. And Jack Kennedy was television's darling. Blessed with youth, good looks, a ringing voice, a ready wit, and a keen sense of language, he had made the medium his own. His image was etched in the nation's memory, his voice echoed in its ears. On the flickering stage in every living room, he was a tough act to follow.

Television and the LBJ style were ill matched. Johnson spoke with a drawl, engaging enough in person but alien to an ear tuned to the unaccented voices of newscasters. Part of his style lay in movement and gesture, but televised speeches required that he stay fixed behind a podium. Time constraints limited the use of the rambling plain-spoken anecdotes that so enlivened his stump speeches and conversations. Concern for the president's security cautioned against mingling with crowds and even, it was said, hanging a lavaliere microphone from his neck.

Television is a folksy medium, the speaker a visitor in your living room. An interviewee ought to be chatty and witty, casual in speech and dress. Johnson had wit but not glibness; he was too focused to be chatty, too conscious of his office to be casual. Oddly, the camera often would some-how transform his grimace into a smile and his smile into a smirk. Those who tutor a person on how to appear on television will counsel, "Just be yourself, let the camera do the work." The camera never worked for Lyn-don Johnson.

Though his style might not carry over, words still mattered to Johnson. He had admired the superb orations of his predecessor and had a high re-gard for his speechwriters. When LBJ took office, he asked that Kennedy's writers stay on. Some did and served the new administration well. In time, though, personal loyalties and new opportunities took some of them elsewhere.

Johnson also recruited his own speechwriters. Some came from within the administration, others from the private sector. All had professional reputations but were largely unknown to the public. This was as LBJ wanted it. He would tell his writers, "No right-thinking American be-lieves that his busy president sits down late at night and writes all his own speeches. But we don't have to remind him of that. I don't want to see your name in the paper. I don't want you talking to reporters or colum-nists. I don't want to read about you jumping into some swimming pool out in Georgetown, with or without your clothes on. You serve best when no one knows who you are or what you do here."

Speech writing is rightly called ghostwriting. The professional writer should have a decent hesitance to speak to others of shared confidences or to make light of the grammatical or rhetorical shortcomings of the speaker. It ill becomes a writer to seek even vicarious credit for a well-turned phrase or historic utterance. This is especially important in government, where the speaker's persona can affect the people's confi-dence, and ultimately on the public good. History indeed must be served, but is better written by those who make it than by those who merely articulate it.

It has been said that policy makers make speeches and speechwriters make policy. In any administration, everybody wants to be a speechwriter, or at least to have some input into what the president is saying. Johnson welcomed and often solicited these contributions, from people both within and outside the White House. For important occasions, he would weigh several drafts, picking, choosing, blending, adding or discarding.

The annual State of the Union Address is the prime example. The whole administration is called upon for input. Each cabinet officer is expected and eager to detail the successes and initiatives in his area. These are submitted long before and are argued over, lobbied for, honed down, and finally incorporated into what is usually a dull and overlong speech. Yet the occasion has drama, and the address can be of great significance.

In the latter years of the Johnson administration, there were four— again the magic word—assistants charged solely with drafting remarks suitable for all the president's public appearances. These were many, perhaps two or three on a given day, several a week, and hundreds a year. They ranged, of course, from the State of the Union and other significant addresses to Congress down through televised speeches, bill signings in the East Room, appearances before prestigious audiences, arrival and departure statements at airports, and remarks to small groups in the Rose Garden.

Johnson had put in place an elaborate process for the preparation of all his remarks. Late in each week, the speechwriters would review the president's calendar for the coming week. The occasions and remarks deemed appropriate for each audience would be divvied up according to each writer's interests, experience, and areas of specialty: education or the arts, crime or urban affairs, poverty, civil rights, the environment (we called it "conservation" then), and campaign matters and politics. Little premium was put on originality or pride of authorship; there was much rewriting of previous remarks, and much helping out of one another.

Especially for the major talks, the appropriate cabinet office or agency would be asked to forward a rough draft covering its concerns or need for pending legislation, and it was usually requested for the next day. The White House writer would rewrite and shorten the draft to fit "the president's style." Sometimes, the president or a member of his staff would convey directly the points to be made. But even absent this, there was little doubt as to what was on the president's mind or what he would want to say. He made no secret of his wishes. The draft would be carefully fact-checked, run back through the interested agency, typed as a reading text, and sent to the president, very often only the day or the night before.

Then he had three options, all of which he frequently exercised. He could conclude the speech was worthless; he would call the writer (or often one of the others, and often at home), pronounce the speech no damn good, and order up another version for first thing in the morning. Or he could decide not to attend the function, or to send a replacement to read the worthless speech, or whatever else the understudy wanted to deliver. Or, more often, he would take the text, use only the portions he liked, and ad-lib the rest.

Lyndon Johnson was masterful at this. His ad-libs were almost always superior to what had been prepared. He had a gift of being able to depart from the text, extemporize for many minutes, and then go back without skipping a beat or repeating himself. Later, he was not above calling the writer's attention to which parts had drawn the most applause or had got the most coverage in the press.

In fairness, it might be noted that at times LBJ's ad-libs brought trouble. Once, while addressing our troops in South Korea, his exuberance caused him to tell them that one of his ancestors had died at the Alamo. This was widely reported, and the press wondered exactly which ancestor that had been. It turned out that no Johnson was inscribed in the role of heroes in that hallowed place. All this caused some consternation in the press office. The speechwriters were blamed. The White House archivist was at a loss as to how it should be handled in the Public Papers. Thought was even given to dispatching someone to San Antonio to chisel in a Johnson. It was finally concluded that the president had "misspoken." The "credibility gap" sadly widened.

Jokes had a place in some public appearances. Lyndon Johnson was a wonderful storyteller. He loved a funny story, and he would deliver it with relish and usually enlarge upon it with each telling. The comedian's one-liners, however, were not his forte. Although any light remark that a president might make will be received as hilarious, it was acknowledged that a few topical, seemingly extemporaneous, jokes at the beginning of a talk served to relax both the speaker and his audience.

LBJ commissioned his writers to submit a string of jokes, or at least light remarks, as a preface to his public speeches. Joke writing is not an easy task and is best done by committee. The writers would convene informally on late Friday afternoons, address themselves to the coming week's calendar, and set down what might be taken as humorous by the particular audience. Yet despite his legendary sense of humor, LBJ very often would simply not get the joke. "This is funny?" on the margin of a draft proved the benefit of jokes by committee.

By the powers vested in him, a president can solemnly proclaim that throughout the nation a month, a week, or a day is to be designated in honor of some item or event. Even such mundane opportunities for communication did not escape LBJ's attention. Early in his administration, he concluded that the "Whereas" that introduced each paragraph in such documents was superfluous. It was duly stricken from all future LBJ proclamations. This made them briefer, hence better.

In 1966, Thanksgiving Day was to be proclaimed, as it had been by every president since Lincoln. A draft was sent to the president for signature. He fired it off to his speechwriters, saying it had no merit, especially because it did not remind the nation of all the blessings for which it could be thankful, among them some of the early fruits of the Great Society.

The Thanksgiving Proclamation was duly rewritten. Drafted just a day after the four-four-four lecture, it was couched in the newly prescribed style. It began, "They came in tiny wooden ships. They settled and survived." It went on to enumerate—albeit not briefly—all the nation's blessings. It was sent to the president and forgotten about.

LBJ was in the Far East when the proclamation was published and was immediately lambasted by an unfriendly New York columnist. He saw it as a desecration of the national holiday, a blatant self-serving campaign document intended solely to garner Democratic votes in the upcoming off-year election. Back in the States, after rereading the proclamation, a delighted president said, "It was damn good." Four words.

In 1964, in an eloquent commencement speech at the University of Michigan, Lyndon Johnson first publicly introduced the lofty goals of the Great Society. "But most of all, the Great Society is not a safe harbor, a resting place, a final objective, a finished product. It is a challenge constantly renewed, beckoning us toward a destiny where the meaning of our lives matches the marvelous products of our labor."

"The Great Society"—a single phrase, first enunciated in a public speech. No less than the New Deal, the Fair Deal, or the New Frontier, it would become the signature of a presidency. It was not immediately seen as that, but in time that ceremony a generation ago would become a historic occasion. It marked the commencement not only of a class but of a mighty work that would transform American life for the better in the final third of a century and into another millennium.

Would such an event, such a speech, such a phrase, be noted today? It is doubtful. We live in an information age, yet the communication of ideas has become more difficult. Words, which mattered so to LBJ, have been drowned out by images. He valued brevity but could not have dealt with a ten-second sound bite. The public's present trivialization of national concerns, its worrying more about secondhand smoke than the survival of its young, could not encompass the breadth of LBJ's goals. Its worship of celebrity allows little room to respect political leadership. Its shortened attention span denies it the broad focus to address either the nation's problems or its progress.

Witness the press. Statistics are factoids. News stories are shortened and headlines enlarged. Witness television, the keen assessor and arbiter of the public's interests. Speeches are sound bites, journalism is entertainment, and news is tabloid. Witness the fact that some networks elect to tape-delay the State of the Union rather than reschedule a situation comedy.

America has changed since the 1960s. That so much of the change is for the better can be traced to Lyndon Johnson. He succeeded in wakening the nation's conscience to our shortcomings, and his Great Society leads us still to their alleviation. Where he failed was to gain victory in Vietnam. That conflict can be seen now as an awful lost battle in a Cold War, that "long twilight struggle" that America would go on to win only a full quarter of a century later.

By 1968, he knew that time was passing him by. On the evening of March 31, in a televised address from his office, he inserted a momentous announcement near the end of his speech. He said, "I shall not seek, and will not accept, the nomination of my party for another term as your president." One sentence, nineteen words, that stunned the world and saddened his friends.

It was a statement that he had told very few people about. That Sunday afternoon he had called his old friend Horace Busby to the White House to write those sad, sad words. To the very close of his presidency, to Lyndon Johnson, words mattered.

# King of the Hill, the Great Coalition Builder: Johnson and Congress

No modern president entered the White House with more national political experience than Lyndon Johnson. He used his background to his advantage and displayed endless energy and persuasive skill in courting allies, neutralizing enemies, forging compromises among conflicting interests, and achieving legislative results. He gave congressional relations the highest priority, completely immersing himself and his staff in the details of legislation. "There is but one way for a president to deal with Congress," Johnson believed, "and that is continuously, incessantly, and without interruption." "If it is really going to work," Johnson said, "the relationship between the president and Congress has got to be almost incestuous. . . . He's got to know them better," he continued, "than they know themselves." Clearly his methods worked, as few presidents can match his legislative success. Sherwin J. Markman examines the masterful skills and methods he employed with Congress to accomplish his domestic agenda. Will we ever see another president able to work so closely and successfully with Congress?

# Making Friends in Congress:
# LBJ and Congressional Relations
## *Sherwin J. Markman*

"Each and every one of you will make friends in Congress. Not just professional relationships but warm and personal friendships. Meet their wives and children. Invite them home for dinner. Get to know them well. Most of all, let them know that you are someone they can immediately call upon for any problem they have with the government. You will work that problem and, if at all possible, solve it for them. Then, when the time comes that you need their vote on something I want from Congress, they will be inclined to help you out in any way they can."

With these instructions, insistently given and often repeated in words very much like those, Lyndon Johnson pounded his method of dealing with Congress into everyone who worked for him. There were no exceptions. Regardless of rank or pecking order, all of us were given these marching orders. The entire membership of the House and Senate, Democrats and Republicans alike, was included. Everyone on the White House staff followed these orders, and the results can be quantified by the sheer number of historic laws enacted. That is not to say that there was any less partisanship during the years of the Johnson presidency but that it was dramatically different from the strife and uncontrolled personal attacks that we see today. Such things existed, but they were muted, and there was always room for reasonable compromise. During the years of Lyndon Johnson's presidency there was a sense of mutual respect and a willingness to get things done. Civility was not lost even during the bitter disagreements over matters such as the war in Vietnam. In my opinion, the special relationship between Lyndon Johnson and the Congress, fostered in significant measure by his orders to his staff, was the core genius of his presidency.

There was a congressional liaison staff at the White House, and for a time I was a part of it. Larry O'Brien led that staff, as he had when John Kennedy was president. As a matter of fact, Johnson considered O'Brien so effective at his White House job that even as Postmaster General he continued acting as Johnson's chief lobbyist, to the extent of retaining his White House office. O'Brien was one of the few persons close to John Kennedy who stayed on to help Lyndon Johnson—and for that act of loyalty to the presidency he suffered painful vilification from many of Kennedy's friends who never forgave him for his perceived "disloyalty" to the martyred president. O'Brien did not see it that way. He believed that his close relationship with so many congressmen and senators—plus the fact that he carried so much of the Kennedy aura—enabled him to perform an invaluable service to his country.

In addition, each and every department and agency was required to organize a full-time staff dedicated to fostering close working relationships with members of Congress who were relevant to their particular programs. The work of each of those congressional relations offices was closely supervised and coordinated by O'Brien. He held regularly scheduled White House meetings where they all reported and were given their marching orders. It was a highly effective operation.

Lyndon Johnson never lost his focus on the vital importance of working with Congress, and he and everyone under him knew that "working with Congress" meant much more than simply lobbying for votes. To my mind, this was the most unique imprint that Lyndon Johnson brought to the presidency, the one that separates him from all other occupants of that office. Of course, other presidents had congressional backgrounds—think of Gerald Ford, Richard Nixon, John Kennedy, Harry Truman, and others more distantly removed. But none of them had the laser-beam focus on the Congress that was the essence of Lyndon Johnson. This was because Lyndon Johnson was a creature of the Congress, immersed in and totally conversant with its ways.

Johnson's knowledge of the arcane ways of Congress was buttressed by his close friendships with so many of its members. Lyndon and Lady Bird

Johnson were contemporaries of a large number of members and their spouses, with whom they had long shared the joys and tribulations of congressional life in Washington. That, in turn, was overlaid by Johnson's intimate understanding of the likes, dislikes, strengths, weaknesses, and needs of an amazing number of senators and congressmen, both Democrats and Republicans. It was his not so secret weapon, and one that he was never reluctant to use.

Those friendships were unhesitatingly used by Johnson to press forward with his program—although not all of them survived to the end of his presidency. A sad example of one that did not was what happened between the Johnsons and the Fulbrights. Despite the differences in their backgrounds, Lyndon and Lady Bird Johnson had long been intimate friends with William and Betty Fulbright. Their relationship was rock solid at the beginning of the Johnson presidency, and it even survived Johnson's civil rights program, of which Senator Fulbright never fully approved. However, as our involvement in Vietnam grew, Fulbright's opposition to it grew apace until he, as chairman of the Senate Foreign Relations Committee, became one of the leading voices in opposition to that war. On that issue his and the president's relationship—and their friendship—shattered. Much later, when Senator Fulbright joined my law firm, with an office next to mine, he often ruminated sadly that he and his wife had irretrievably lost the friendship of the Johnsons because of the depth of their disagreement over the Vietnam War.

Yet through good times and bad, Lyndon Johnson never ceased working with Congress. He had gained a well-deserved reputation as perhaps the most effective majority leader in the history of the Senate. That reputation was built upon two footings: he could "count heads," meaning that he knew where every senator stood on every important issue; and he was a renowned "arm twister," meaning that he also knew the best way to approach each senator. Television was never able to capture his skill in persuading individuals or his effectiveness in communicating with small groups. Nonetheless, as I often observed, his skill in those circumstances was impressive and unsurpassed.

When a matter before Congress was important to him and the vote was going to be close, the president without hesitation personally took up the cudgels and joined the fight. Most often he did so by telephone calls to members while Larry O'Brien, sitting at his side, guided the president from an exceedingly accurate list showing where each member stood on the issue. Adjusting his manner to the individual to whom he was speaking, Johnson would tirelessly plead, cajole, flatter, or even threaten until, more often than not, he received the commitment he sought. Many times he invited the members of Congress to the White House, sometimes one at a time, more usually in small groups, with whom he would sit convivially around the table in the cabinet room or on the couches in the Oval Office. There the president confidently presided and, his words interspersed with wit and satire, worked his audience until they were his. To those who knew and worked with him, it was a tragedy that this Lyndon Johnson could never be projected to the public at large.

Lyndon Johnson had many means by which he imposed his will upon the Congress; let me cite one critical example. One of the major civil rights bills was about to come to the floor of the Senate. Larry O'Brien's careful vote count showed that although a majority of senators favored the legislation, that majority fell a few votes short of the 60 percent needed to forestall the inevitable southern filibuster that would kill the legislation. In this instance, that minority also contained many Republican senators who had allied themselves with the southern Democrats. Johnson knew there was no way he could squeeze out any more Democratic votes; his only hope was to wean the votes he needed from the Republicans. In order to accomplish this, Johnson had to go to his old adversary—and good friend—Everett Dirkson, the Republican leader in the Senate.

Johnson asked Dirkson what it would take for him to deliver the votes of enough Republican senators to block the impending filibuster. Dirkson responded by presenting a "shopping list" of what he wanted—that is, particular federal programs for Illinois (his home state), and a decisive voice in certain presidential appointees from Illinois, such as judges. Dirkson's list was negotiated; a compromise agreement was reached; Dirkson delivered the necessary votes; the filibuster was broken; and the civil rights legislation was enacted into law. Later, Johnson saw to it that his administration carried out his part of the bargain.

It is likely that if the same scenario were repeated now, it would be leaked to the press, or some enterprising reporter would ferret out the story, which would be published to an outcry of dismay from countless editorial writers and television commentators. Accusations of unethical conduct, even bribery, might fill the air. Perhaps a special prosecutor would be appointed, or, at a minimum, a congressional investigation would ensue. Most certainly, the result would damage everyone who had participated in the arrangement. Yet that was how it was done, and who can say that the country is not better off for it? We definitely thought it was at the time.

Lyndon Johnson's view of the importance of Congress, especially powerful committee chairmen, was not always fully appreciated by members of his staff. In one painful instance, that included me. It happened while I was in Paris attending a reception hosted by our ambassador for important members of the French government, as well as for several members of Congress and myself. One of the congressmen was Wayne Hayes, a powerful and (as all who dealt with him knew) very nasty committee chairman. On this occasion, Congressman Hayes was very drunk, his words slurred. He was loudly excoriating the president, accusing him of incompetence, stupidity, and misconduct. He would not stop, and his audience of French officials was shocked and embarrassed. Finally, I could take it no more. I stepped in and introduced myself as a member of the president's staff. I told him I thought that he was being unfair to the president, and that it was wrong of him to be speaking as he was in a foreign capital to a foreign group. Hayes, red faced and angry, told me to go to hell.

Later, asleep in my room, the telephone rang. It was Hayes. He proceeded to tell me that he would not forget what I had said to him earlier and that as soon as he returned to Washington he was going to call the president and have me fired. He sounded as if he was still drunk; I hoped his threat would vanish in the morning. It did not, because the day I returned to the White House, I was summoned to the Oval Office. The president asked me what had happened between Hayes and me, because Hayes had just called him, demanding my head. I explained that I had tried to defend the president from an inexcusable attack by a drunken congressman. The president shook his head and said that although he appreciated my loyalty, I was dead wrong to antagonize a powerful committee chairman and that as difficult as it might be, I must go to Hayes's office and apologize. With great reluctance, I did just that. Swallowing my pride, I met with Hayes and told him how wrong I had been and how much I regretted what I had done. Hayes sat there, triumphantly smiling. When I finished, he told me that he thought I showed great character in coming to him as I had, and that he forgave me. It was a humiliating experience, but the result was that a powerful House member was retained as a supporter of the Johnson program. After my apology, Hayes always treated me well, although his reputation as a bully never changed. Much later, Hayes was brought down by a personal scandal, which gave me no satisfaction, only sadness.

Lyndon Johnson had other ways of dealing with the Congress, some of them too subtle for me to understand immediately. The following experience is illustrative. It was the Christmas season of 1966 and the Congress had adjourned until January. The normally hectic pace at the White House had slowed to a pleasant and welcome crawl. One afternoon, in a meeting with some of us on his staff, the president mentioned that it would be a good thing if one or more of us tried personally to learn more about what was happening in the inner cities. If anyone was interested, they should talk to him about it. I immediately volunteered, and he told me to stay with him after the meeting.

I followed him into the Oval Office, and he waved to me to sit down before he said, "What I want is for you to go live inside an inner-city ghetto."

"I don't understand," I stammered.

"You heard me right. You go out and live in the worst Negro ghetto you can find. I think Chicago would be good. And I don't want you checking into some hotel and commuting back and forth. I want you to plunk yourself down inside the ghetto and live there day and night. Keep your eyes and ears open. Stay there ten days or two weeks, long enough to learn which of my programs are working and which aren't—and why. Tell me who the good leaders are and what they're doing. And I want to know about this 'black power' business that is getting people all excited. Then you come back here and give me a written report about what you learned."

I was shocked at what he was asking me to do. "But, Mr. President," I said. "I am white, from the Midwest, and have zero experience with the inner cities."

"That's exactly why you are good for this job," he replied. "I am surrounded by experts, all I ever want. They all have their ideas, and a lot of them are good. But right now I am looking for something else. I need someone whose mind is unpolluted and who I can trust. Just you go out there and look and learn."

I was still bewildered. "How am I supposed to do what you want?"

"I think you're smart enough to figure it out," he said, brushing aside my question. "Just don't you get into any trouble while you're living out there; don't get your name in the newspaper; and don't let anyone know you are from the White House. Do you understand?"

"Yes, sir," I said, with as much lack of confidence as I felt.

Back in my office, I tried to think of how to carry out the president's wishes. It was obvious that there was no way I simply could march into the heart of Chicago's ghetto in the dead of winter. I needed help from someone black who was familiar with the worst parts of Chicago—someone who was smart, imaginative, and, above all, trustworthy. But nobody I knew met those requirements. Despite some nervousness because of the president's admonition that he wanted nothing to appear in the press, I telephoned my close friend, Nick Kotz, then a reporter with the Washington bureau of my hometown newspaper, the *Des Moines Register*. Off the record, I told him the whole story and asked if he knew anyone who might go with me. As it turned out, he did. He suggested Ken Vallis, a good friend of his who was working at the Department of Labor in Washington. Ken had been born and raised in the Chicago ghetto and had the intelligence and drive to rise despite every conceivable obstacle. Nick introduced me to Ken, and in mid-January the two of us flew into cold and snowy Chicago.

Chicago had two separate ghetto areas, one in the south side near the University of Chicago, and the other in the much rougher west side of the city. Ken and I spent some time examining the south side ghetto, but, carrying out the president's directive that I was not to commute in and out of the ghetto, he and I drove to the west side, where we moved in with a friend of his who had a small apartment with room enough for us to share a bedroom. For ten days and late into each night, Ken and I visited as many anti-poverty projects as time allowed, had lengthy conversations with community leaders and activists, and walked the streets talking to as many ordinary people as possible. The president had also ordered me not to reveal where I worked, so we concocted a cover story identifying me as a representative from Sargent Shriver's Office of Economic Opportunity. I don't know if anyone was fooled by this, but I avoided getting into trouble, and nothing appeared in the press.

Those days in Chicago with Ken Vallis were a revelation to me—and an education. I found myself living in a world totally occupied by African Americans. I was the only white person around, but people did open up to us, and I saw, I listened, and I learned. When we finished, although I was still no expert, I was overflowing with impressions and ideas.

I left Chicago in the midst of its worst blizzard in years, one that shut down all transportation in the city. Ken decided to stay on with his family, but I managed to trudge through several miles of snow to the railroad station, where I was lucky to find a seat on the only train going east toward Washington. I did not sleep on the overnight journey. Instead, I spent the time pouring out my thoughts in a memorandum for the president. When I finally arrived at the White House and had it typed, I was shocked to see that it was over ten pages long—and single-spaced at that. The president, who was inundated with so much reading material that he was required to take massive amounts of it to his bedroom each night, had warned all of us that he wanted all messages to him to be brief. My memorandum definitely did not fit that criterion.

My first instinct was to cut my report—drastically. But if I did that, then I could not adequately describe the terrible conditions I saw or express the depth of my reaction to them. Also lost would be descriptions of which of the president's programs were working, which were not, and why. Most importantly, I would be omitting my observations of the good people out there on the firing line effectively fighting his War on Poverty. So, very nervous about his reaction, I delivered my unexpurgated report to him.

Then I waited. I was sure there would be an explosion because of my utter disregard of the president's standing order on length. But nothing happened. For days, then weeks, I heard nothing, neither blame nor approval. Only silence. I assumed that my memorandum had not been read or had been shunted off to some department or another. I was not about to ask, and I was secretly relieved that I seemed to have dodged an outburst of presidential wrath.

Over a month later, I learned the president's purpose for sending me into the ghetto and requiring a written report. One of the president's important anti-poverty bills was in trouble in the House of Representatives. The key to its passage lay in the votes of a score of undecided Democrats. On this day, all of these men had been invited to the White House to meet with the president. They were seated around the cabinet table as the president spoke about the importance of the legislation.

Then, with no preamble, the president reached into the inside pocket of his suit jacket, pulled out a sheaf of papers, unfolded them, and began to read aloud. To my amazement, he was reading from the part of my ghetto memorandum that described the abject poverty I had seen and my frustration over the fact that I believed we could relieve these conditions but were failing to do so. After reading a few paragraphs, the president paused and, fixing his gaze on the members seated around the table, declared that what he was reading was not a report from some bureaucrat or left-wing do-gooder but a personal memorandum to him from a white, conservative (I shuddered a bit at this), midwesterner who was a member of his staff (I was relieved that he did not identify me). Then he returned to reading from my memorandum. Finally, the president told them that if his man could see things the way he did, then they should be able to do the same. I detected no particular reaction from the congressmen. I like to believe, however, because most of those present ultimately voted for the legislation (and it became law), that what he had had me do for him was of some small assistance in his War on Poverty.

What is clear is that part of the president's motive in sending someone like me into the Chicago ghetto was to create a tool he could use to help him influence congressmen—an illustration of Lyndon Johnson's imaginative, effective, innovative, and unique method of dealing with Congress.

A further illustration of a dividend reaped because of how President Johnson used his staff in dealing with Congress is the story of Congresswoman Julia Butler Hanson and me. As I have written, he directed each of us to make friends—close friends, if at all possible—with as many senators and congressmen as possible. One member I came to know very well was Congresswoman Hanson. Julia was a unique woman. She had published several books of children's poetry, had been the Democratic leader in the Washington State Senate, and now chaired the House subcommittee on Appropriations, which controlled the funding for federal cultural projects. She was the first woman member to occupy such a powerful position. She had a deserved reputation as exceedingly tough minded, although, as I discovered, her hardboiled exterior masked great personal warmth and sensitivity. She was also a devout Christian Scientist with a taste for leisurely three martini lunches, which never seemed to affect her—although I cannot claim the same for me. I came to know her well, and she in turn called me "her man in the White House."

Our friendship had a rocky start. I first met Julia on a trip to South America, where I had been detailed to escort her and a Republican member of the House Appropriations Committee, which was then considering funding for the Alliance for Progress, a John Kennedy–inspired program to provide financial aid to our Latin American neighbors. In the middle of the trip, I contracted dysentery and was badly in need of medication to keep on going. However, Julia, good Christian Scientist that she was, all but ordered me to abjure all drugs (except for joining with her daily for martinis). I, believing that my duty to placate her overrode the needs of my suffering body, went along with her prescribed therapy—forcing myself forward while silently cursing her for denying me medication. Somehow I survived the ordeal, and my anger at her not only abated but changed to become a warm friendship that endured and grew during the ensuing years.

Julia was a solid liberal whose votes for the president's anti-poverty programs were never in doubt. Likewise, she became a strong supporter of the Alliance for Progress. So lobbying for her vote was never necessary. For years, our relationship was strictly a one-way street—whenever she had a problem anywhere in the executive branch she would call me, and I would then do my best (usually successfully) to resolve it.

The one and only time I was required to impose upon our friendship came in the summer of 1968. It had been a very hard year. On March 31, the president announced that he was not running for reelection, thus diminishing his ability to influence the Congress. Martin Luther King and Bobby Kennedy had been assassinated. Riots were tearing apart our cities. Hubert Humphrey was trying to pull the Democratic Party out of chaos. And the Vietnam War showed no sign of abating. In the midst of all of that, Roger Stevens was struggling to find the funds to build the Kennedy Center, but that funding was being held up in the House of Representatives. More specifically, Julia Butler Hanson was blocking it in her capacity as chair of the relevant subcommittee. Unable to persuade her, Stevens appealed to the president for help. The president, knowing that I had spent years building a strong relationship with Julia, sent Stevens to me.

Stevens came to my office and explained the problem. I immediately telephoned Julia, and she asked me to come up to the Hill and have lunch with her. That lunch was the usual leisurely multi-martini affair during which I explained to her how important the completion of the Kennedy Center was to the president. At first, she was adamantly negative, calling it a waste of the taxpayers' money. But I continued to press her. Finally, I told her that though I could not remember a single instance where I had asked her to change her position on any legislation, I definitely was doing that now. In the end, she said, "If you tell me the president really wants the money for this project, then I will see to it that he gets it." That was all it took. She unblocked the appropriation, and after that it sailed through Congress, a crucial step toward the magnificent reality the Kennedy Center is today.

The foregoing illustrates the farsighted wisdom of Lyndon Johnson's standing order to his staff: form close personal friendships with members of Congress; be there for them all the time; and when the day comes when you truly need them, they will be there for you.

Today, public opinion holds Congress in very low esteem, much lower than the presidency. Despite the weaknesses and peccadilloes of current and recent occupants of the White House, the great majority of Americans retain a high opinion of that office. The difference in how the two institutions are viewed by the public, however vast, is no excuse for any president to ignore, denigrate, or otherwise attempt to beat up the Congress. By and large, a president should resist the temptation of using his "bully pulpit"—always incomparably greater than that of any member of Congress, however well known—to attack Congress. Moreover, a president should use his powers, and those that devolve to members of his staff, to foster lines of civil communication with members from both political parties. Lyndon Johnson was a master at this. I do not recall a more bilious atmosphere between the president and the Congress than that which existed in the Clinton administration. What is clear to me is that Lyndon Johnson would never have allowed such deterioration to occur. He knew that to govern effectively, to move the nation forward, to get his core beliefs enacted into law, the president must work with and not against the Congress. That requires paying constant attention to the cares, needs, beliefs, and egos of each and every senator and representative. President Johnson did that, and the people of the United States were the beneficiaries.

# "I Envision an America Where . . .": Domestic Problems and the War on Poverty

Johnson's programs have shaped the national agenda for the past thirty-five years and have left a complicated legacy. Ervin Duggan, Hyman Bookbinder, and Larry Levinson ask what aspects of specific programs in which they participated succeeded or failed, and why. They each raise such questions as: Was Johnson's vision for a "Great Society" possible? Can a society adopt a broad reform agenda—one that affects many particular groups—and still maintain a consensus? Should, or can, the federal government really do anything significant to remedy pervasive social problems? Did societal change occur so rapidly that the legislative machinery and federal government were unable to keep pace? Most importantly, can Great Society–type programs reinvent themselves and solve persistent problems that went unsolved thirty years ago, or should we abandon the course today? A constantly recurring theme in almost every analysis of Lyndon Johnson's "War on Poverty" is the deadly effect of the war in Vietnam. That war divided America more than any other event in the twentieth century; it undeniably damaged, perhaps destroyed, Johnson's ability to enact the legislation and, more importantly, to secure the funding that was the lifeblood of his programs. Yet despite full knowledge of what the war was doing to his presidency, Johnson persisted with its prosecution. It is appropriate therefore to conclude an examination of the Great Society with an essay by Peter Rosenblatt that, even today, defends the Vietnam War and by so doing sheds light upon why Johnson would not, or could not, abandon it regardless of its cost in lives, treasure, and his dreams.

# Sending the Whole Country to Harvard: Lyndon Johnson's Education Revolution
## Ervin S. Duggan

Looking back, reasonable people have disagreed on the exact number of education laws Lyndon Johnson placed on the books. The number of acts he got passed ranges anywhere from sixty to a hundred, depending on the source of information. The uncertainty has a lot to do with the vagueness of categories. The Health Professions Educational Assistance Act of 1965, for instance, could rightfully be counted as either an education measure or health-care legislation. Moreover, the creation of the National Endowment for the Humanities could be classified as "education" legislation or fall into other categories, depending upon one's perspective.

But let us forgo hairsplitting. However we enumerate his legislative achievements, LBJ's educational legacy is monumental. The effects and impact of his educational programs today remain wide, sweeping, and permanently embedded in, and tightly woven into, the cultural fabric of American life. Sixty percent of today's college and university students, for example, receive some sort of federal grant or loan from programs traceable to Great Society legislation. As former LBJ aide Joe Califano asked rhetorically in a memorable speech in 1999, "If Johnson's revolution had not established the federal government's responsibility to finance this educational surge, would the U. S. have had the trained human resources to be the world's greatest industrial power today? Would the U. S.  be the

leading power in computer and information and technology?" The answer to each of these questions is a resounding "no."

When we look at the background against which LBJ worked and
fought, Califano's use of the word "revolution" seems appropriate. There
was little or no precedent for involving the federal government in education; education in America had been, by long tradition, the province of
state and local government. Among Johnson's predecessors, Dwight
Eisenhower had achieved a small program of graduate-school loans and
grants, using Cold War tensions to push through a National Defense Education Act. But that was about it. Significant federal aid to local schools,
which Harry Truman had vainly proposed nearly two decades before, was
still considered an impossible dream when LBJ won his landslide in 1964.

Republicans during the period stoutly opposed increasing the federal
role in education. Many southern Democrats, still resisting the integration of public schools and the broader civil rights movement, were not
eager to invite the federal government any farther into the arena of education. Finally, the Gordian knot of church-state politics also seemed impossible to cut. The Roman Catholic hierarchy in the United States
determined that if public schools received federal aid, Catholic parochial
schools also were entitled to assistance. For their part, many concerned
Protestants and many constitutional scholars argued against that position
and threatened the hallowed principle of church-state separation.

In short, LBJ faced an uphill political road. An unlikely coalition of allies, conservative Republicans, Southern Democrats, and urban Catholic
liberals, attempted to block any new education legislation that did not
protect their respective interests. That marriage of allies, for all its odd-
ness, seemed big enough and strong enough to prevent the passage of
meaningful federal education legislation.

In the end, these obstacles mattered little. Johnson not only proved a
master of the "art of the possible" but changed the very limits of possibili-
ties. Johnson mobilized teachers' groups and education associations into a
powerful counter-coalition, through a variety of strategies. He skillfully
tied school aid to his War on Poverty (Title I of his elementary-secondary
school bill was aimed at "educationally disadvantaged" pupils and school
districts). He horse-traded with his potential opponents. He set off with
the National Conference of Catholic Bishops a round of negotiations that
created a complicated formula designed to accomplish the impossible. He
resourcefully defused the Catholic Church's concerns about the equity of

his education programs by including parochial school students in the new legislation's benefits. His prescription for education passed constitutional muster and somehow managed to avoid setting off a firestorm among conservative Protestants. Johnson proved once again to be the master of compromise. "Have you ever noticed," a colleague once remarked to LBJ's chief education aide, Douglass Cater, "that if the bishops come to the Cabinet Room on Wednesday, . . . the president invites Billy Graham to the White House for the weekend?"

The only explosive reaction was a flurry of "impossible" education laws. Important, though lesser, laws, followed the significant Elementary and Secondary Education Act of 1965. The momentous Higher Education Act of 1965 created a far-reaching system of student grants and loans (and required complicated negotiations with the banking industry). Johnson also passed bills to build new college and university facilities; for awhile in the mid-sixties, new community colleges were founded across the nation at a rate of one a month.

Seeing that kindergarten and early-childhood education were common in affluent neighborhoods but not among the poor, Johnson engineered the Head Start Program, another education program linked to his War on Poverty. Taking inspiration from the Peace Corps, Johnson also proposed, and got, a Teacher Corps, which sent its teacher volunteers into resource-starved schools in Appalachia, in urban ghettos, and on Indian reservations. There was a bilingual-education act for immigrant children and a special education act for disabled students. Taking inspiration from the original GI Bill, Johnson pushed through Congress a Vietnam-era GI Bill; at the signing ceremony, tears glinting on their cheeks, stood scores of congressmen who poignantly credited their careers to the original GI Bill.

Johnson sponsored White House conferences on education, staged Rose Garden bill-signing ceremonies crowded with educators and members of Congress, and toured the country trumpeting, on college campuses and in front of schoolhouses, the cause of education for everyone. In every one of these appearances, he ad-libbed a philosophy that was startling to some but was pure, unadulterated LBJ: "We're gonna give every boy and girl in America," he said, "rich or poor, black or white, *all the education he or she can take!*"

The three-year torrent of education legislation included laws not only directly aiding schools, colleges, and students but aimed at enhancing the general culture. Important examples are the creation of the John F. Kennedy Center in Washington as a national center for the performing arts, the establishment of arts and humanities endowments, the founding of the Woodrow Wilson Center for Scholars, and passage of the Public Broadcasting Act of 1967, which provided federal support for public television and radio stations.

Johnson's legislative opponents—outnumbered, outgunned, and outmaneuvered—were outraged. Fiscal conservatives yelped that the new federal education outlays would bankrupt the treasury. Social conservatives predicted that programs like Head Start would wrest young children away from their parental authority and disrupt family life. Critics of the Vietnam War charged that the Vietnam-era GI Bill was cynically designed to lure poor kids into the army. Pedagogical conservatives warned that college grants and loans would create an influx of "unqualified" students onto the nation's campuses and drag down academic quality.

Those concerns never materialized, and in each case the opposite appears to have been true. The results of Johnson's education programs have been as benign as they have been dramatic. Consider only a few statistics. In 1963, when Johnson took office, fewer than half of all Americans (41 percent) had finished high school; by 1998, more than 81 percent were high school graduates. In the early sixties, fewer than 10 percent of Americans were college graduates; today the proportion of college graduates has more than doubled (24 percent). This has surely been due, in part, to student loans, which have benefited twenty-nine million students. Moreover, more than sixteen million children have received preschool education under Head Start, a program that today serves 800,000 children annually. Also, LBJ's Health Professions Educational Assistance Act doubled the number of doctors turned out annually from the nation's medical schools.

Yet Johnson's scores of education laws, to be sure, have created no educational utopia. The nation today, even after spending $120 billion in federal aid to elementary and secondary schools, still struggles with the question of how to guarantee both broad access and high quality in its public schools. It is to Johnson's lasting credit, however, that he declared this double challenge, access *and* quality, not just one or the other, a top priority for a society aspiring to be great.

Surely Joe Califano is right when he asserts that Johnson's revolutionary creation of a major federal role in supporting education played a role in America's national success three decades later. Surely the explosion in educational opportunity created by Johnson's programs plays some role today in the nation's flourishing contemporary achievements.

There are theorists who insist that history is determined by impersonal forces, who reject the notion that persons or personalities shape history in any decisive way. In their view, Lyndon Johnson's education legacy—and indeed his entire domestic record, from Medicare to the Redwoods National Park—can be explained by "objective factors," such as a booming economy, combined with an electoral landslide. Those who watched LBJ at work know differently. Having felt the force of his personality, his insistent, impatient, do-it-all-now personality, they know that Lyndon Johnson's titanic personal impulses as much as any "objective factors" lay at the source of those Great Society achievements.

Perhaps because he had lived through the Depression in the Texas hill country, LBJ had a visceral hatred of material waste. He would wander about the White House snapping off light switches in empty rooms. He hated even more the waste of human energy and human potential. In response, he flayed his aides and his congressional allies into pushing education programs, dozens of them—programs he considered wise investments in human potential.

He had an intense, incurable restlessness that made him always want more, that made it impossible for him to stop wanting, stop working, or stop achieving. In education, as on other fronts, he simply did not accept obstacles that others thought insurmountable. For example, he insisted—restlessly, impatiently, unreasonably—that some workable version of an education bill could be, *must be*, negotiated with the Catholic bishops. His impatience and insistence, not "objective factors," is the reason that it happened.

He had, finally, an immense faith in the curative, empowering magic of education. "Every man," said Schopenhauer, "loves what he lacks." Lyndon Johnson did not lack intelligence, intellectual power, or even sophistication. Virtually everyone who met him saw that he possessed the kind of raw operational genius that can make formal learning seem puny. For him, however, that raw genius was not enough, even though he knew he had it. A part of him, a large part, envied the ease that seemed to come to those who had gone to Groton or Harvard. He loved the sophisticated education that he thought he lacked.

He admired his mother, who was cultivated beyond the standards of her time and neighborhood, and he strongly shared her confidence in the power of education to improve the quality of life. Having served as a teacher to poor Hispanic children in Cotulla, Texas, he understood what lower- and middle-class children would miss if they never had opportunities to go to college. Perhaps because he had not gone to Harvard, and because few Hispanic children and other income groups could afford such a school, Lyndon Johnson wanted to send the whole country symbolically "to Harvard."

At one point in Johnson's campaign to pass more and more education legislation, a newspaper columnist, one who had probably been to both Groton and Harvard, wrote that the president possessed a "naive, utopian faith" in the power of education. Half-believing it himself, Doug Cater mentioned it to LBJ. "Mr. President," he said, "So-and-so says you have a naive, utopian faith that education alone can solve all the country's problems." The president replied with unconcealed sarcasm. "No, Doug," he said, "I don't have any 'naive, utopian faith.' I don't believe that education alone can solve all our problems." He paused, then said softly: "I just believe that without it, we can't solve any of them."

# We Can No Longer Ignore Poverty in Our Midst: LBJ's Other War
## *Hyman Bookbinder*

In an address to a joint session of Congress in March 1965, President Johnson recalled his first job after college, as a teacher in a small Mexican-American school in Catulla, Texas. "Somehow you never forget what poverty and hatred can do when you see its scars on the hopeful face of a young child," he told his former colleagues in the Congress. "I never thought then, in 1928, that I would be standing here, in 1965. It never occurred to me in my fondest dreams that I might someday have the chance to help the sons and daughters of those students and to help people like them." Then he proclaimed, almost defiantly: "But now I do have that chance—and I'll let you in on a secret: I do mean to use it!"

That was no idle threat. It had not taken the new president long to get started on that "fondest dream," something until this point in time he had not dared to dream. On the very first full day of his presidency (as he would vividly recall in his autobiography), he arranged to see that night in the White House Walter Heller, the chairman of the Council of Economic Advisers, who had been waiting anxiously to brief him on a report that had been prepared for John Kennedy and was on the new president's desk, ready for attention.

President Kennedy, Heller explained to President Johnson, "had been so moved by Michael Harrington's book *The Other America* and wanted to understand better just who were these millions of poor Americans, why were they poor, and what could the government do to get them out of poverty, and keep them out of poverty?" Heller's primary answer to these questions was contained in that report on LBJ's desk. Before that first conversation with Heller was over, the new president made what was soon recognized as a historic decision. "This is my undertaking," he told Heller. "I'm interested. I'm sympathetic. Go ahead. Give it the highest priority. Push ahead full tilt."

With the whole myriad of critical demands facing him, domestic and foreign, as he assumed the presidency of the world's leading nation, LBJ had sensed immediately that this challenge of unacceptable levels of poverty in a generally affluent society could and should be the hallmark of his administration. Moreover, he was convinced that no "Great Society," as he would soon be calling his program, could ignore the plight of its most disadvantaged people.

Who were these disadvantaged, these poor? Heller's detailed analysis helped him understand not only the numbers of poor but also their basic characteristics. Among the highlights in that report that influenced the president:

- One-fifth of all American families in 1962 (the last year for which there was reliable data) were poor.
- 9.3 million poor out of forty-seven million families were poor.
- Of the poor, 21 percent were nonwhite, but nearly half of all nonwhite families lived in poverty.
- The heads of families over 60 percent of all poor families had no more than grade-school educations.
- Over 40 percent of farm families were poor.
- One-quarter of all poor families were headed by women, but close to half of all families headed by women were poor.

The most challenging finding in this profile of American poverty was the fact that no less than half of all the poor had been poor from the day they were born. "Breaking the cycle of poverty," not surprisingly, was soon to become the most frequently used formulation of the program's basic goal.

How poor were the poor? Heller's definition, admittedly an arbitrary line, surely could not be faulted for exaggeration. A minimal standard of living for a family of four in the mid-sixties, Heller argued, required a total income from all sources of $3,000 annually. Any family with less income, in an American economy as advanced as it had become, had to be considered "below the poverty line." Helping families get beyond that line and enabling them to stay above it had to be the goals of the new national effort to wipe out poverty.

To be sure that everybody understood the nature and size of this goal, the federal, state, and local governments, industry, labor, and the media needed to be brought together to achieve the end results. LBJ rejected many suggestions for characterizing the proposed program and insisted on calling it a "war on poverty." The name caught on. The country was at war. In more recent years, the designation "war" has been used frequently and with less justification, lowering its public relations value, but at the time it effectively mobilized interest and support.

That initial Johnson/Heller meeting was followed by almost daily working sessions, even through all of Christmas week, that included President Johnson, Walter Heller, Budget Director Kermit Gordon, and a few top officials from key federal agencies. The purpose was to determine the basic outline for the program to be announced to the Congress and the general public. Barely seven weeks into his presidency, a hopeful and proud LBJ felt comfortable and confident enough to pronounce, in his first State of the Union address on January 8, 1964: "This administration, here and now, declares unconditional war on poverty in the United States. . . . It will not be a short or easy struggle, but one which we cannot afford to lose."

With the likely exception of those historic first weeks of Roosevelt's first term in 1933, Washington has never experienced the excitement and anticipations of the week following this "declaration of war." Under the brilliant guidance of Heller and Gordon, a President's Task Force on Poverty, created by executive order since no legislation had yet authorized any program, began exploring ideas until the nuts and bolts of the program could be designed.

LBJ's instincts to trust Heller and Gordon for this major undertaking could not have proven better. I had known them both from my earlier work with the labor movement and then in the Kennedy administration's Commerce Department. They were clearly two of the most respected and knowledgeable professionals the capital had ever seen. They combined impressive economic intelligence with a solid commitment to social justice, exactly the combination the new program needed. They soon attracted scores of additional experts from government agencies and volunteers from universities and the private sector—unfortunately, too numerous to mention here.

A "war" needs a commanding general and command center, and LBJ knew whom and what he wanted. Rejecting early suggestions that the new program be housed in one of the existing federal agencies, LBJ would not yield in his conviction that the new program needed to be part of the Executive Office of the President, with total independence and tough coordinating responsibility. He wanted someone who not only understood government operations but was considered new and fresh, someone unencumbered by bureaucratic inertia. Equally important, he needed someone who could explain and promote the program. His choice from the beginning was Sargent Shriver, the highly acclaimed director of the Kennedy administration's showcase agency, the Peace Corps. Shriver, just home from a long foreign trip on February 1, several weeks after the "declaration of war on poverty," resisted the Johnson appointment; he preferred instead to remain with the Peace Corps. But Johnson was adamant. Shriver (with the inevitable jokes about what kind of war is lead by a "Sergeant?") finally agreed, but only after getting the president's agreement that he could also continue to head the Peace Corps as well.

With the public attention now focused on Shriver's new appointment as director of the Task Force on Poverty, I felt I should call him and offer my congratulations. I had gotten to know him quite well during the 1960 Kennedy campaign. I was personally very pleased about the new program. From my earliest involvement in public affairs, the plight of the disadvantaged had always been a priority interest of mine. At the time, I was in New York, on leave from the Commerce Department, putting together the Eleanor Roosevelt Memorial Foundation. When I asked Shriver on the phone what I could do to help, his answer was curt but one I could not ignore. He replied, "Just get the next shuttle to Washington, and let's talk." Certainly, the last thing on my mind at that time was any interest in changing jobs again, having just moved my family to New York.

The following day I was at Shriver's desk at his Peace Corps headquarters, looking forward to a general discussion of his new responsibilities. In a crowded outer office I saw dozens of young men and women sharing corners of desks, reading and writing memoranda between phone calls. This outer office soon became the first of several temporary headquarters of the President's Task Force on Poverty. Sarge and I talked for less than an hour. By the end of that hour, I agreed to be the executive officer of the task force. I had been swept up in the excitement of the challenge he had laid out. Shriver had now done to me what I was to learn later Johnson did to him.

I recount this personal story because it is not unique. During these task force days and for months after we became an official agency, hundreds of men and women could not resist participating in what they felt was a great and noble cause. Many of them abandoned high-level and prestigious jobs to join the effort. This desire to help, to participate somehow, did not apply only to those seeking or accepting positions within the new program; it applied to the whole range of nongovernment organizations and their representatives from all areas of labor, industry, academia, health, civil rights, education, consumer, and philanthropy.

One of the most critical and memorable aspects of the task force's earliest activities was a series of consultations organized by Shriver, acting on behalf of the president. For ten or more hours every day there was a steady procession of "witnesses," or experts, high-level professionals from nongovernmental organizations. They would sit at one end of a long table, with Shriver and two or three top aides on the other. Each session started with Shriver asking simply: "What would you do if President Johnson had put *you* in charge of a war on poverty?"

The answers were generally, but not always, important and useful. But the real meaning of the exercise went beyond the specifics; it was an invaluable vehicle for challenging every sector of American life to review its own policies and programs for possible change and to enlist their support for the national effort. Later on, each of these sectors was encouraged to participate in the actual programs as they were developed and to help in the political advocacy that was required to get congressional authorization and adequate appropriations. I was privileged to serve later for four years as OEO Assistant Director for Private Groups.

The recommendations from these consultations were forwarded to the task force's legislative drafting team. Senior task force members would meet early every morning with Shriver to review progress and to share concerns about fears and misconceptions that were beginning to surface, from congressional sources, from old-line agencies that felt threatened, from local governments, and from some private social-service organizations.

LBJ was himself concerned with one particular misconception that he felt could arouse serious congressional resistance, namely, that the War on Poverty was really just another civil rights program. As he discussed his proposed program with congressional leaders and others, he artfully exposed the falsity of these ideas and would point out that while black Americans were disproportionately among the poor, four out of every five poor Americans were white.

Perhaps the most critical and persistent misunderstanding about the program was that it would be just another welfare or relief program. The truth was, of course, that while government did indeed have a responsibility to provide aid and comfort to those in distress, the key to LBJ's War on Poverty was his hope to end the cycle of poverty in which in the early sixties too many millions of Americans were trapped.

This was, of course, not the first time the government had taken notice of poverty. In his second inaugural address, for example, Franklin Roosevelt had eloquently cried, "I see one-third of a nation ill housed, ill clad, ill nourished." To relieve such poverty, the New Deal had provided temporary employment opportunities through such programs as the WPA (Works Progress Administration), CCC (Civilian Conservation Corps), and NYA (National Youth Administration). LBJ had himself served as Texas director of the NYA. Many state and local governments had created relief programs during the New Deal to help the poorest of their citizens. The historic Social Security Act of 1935 had provided benefits for those out of work or too old to work.

But never before in our history had a president called for a multipronged effort designed to eliminate the underlying causes of poverty. "Because poverty itself is a complex problem of many interlocking facets," he was to write later, "our assault on it had to be an integrated attack launched on many fronts." No single poverty program could easily reverse centuries of discrimination and deprivation. That reversal would come only with the sustained hard work of dozens of campaigns fought on hundreds of battlegrounds; it would take time.

Proposing rhetorically such a war was relatively easy; administering it was far different. He now had the tough job of choosing those "dozens of campaigns" and "hundreds of battlegrounds" that could be included in legislation to be proposed to the Congress. Numerous difficult choices had to be made. First, the president was certain that the Congress would not approve any more than half a billion dollars in "new money." Second, that modest sum had to be apportioned between the many competing interests and champions of favored programs—in the Congress itself, among the existing federal agencies, and within the private social-service world.

I was, for a short time, personally involved in that competition. When I was persuaded that the decision to limit the first year's budget to that half-billion figure was firm, I wrote a memo to Shriver expressing my view that *all* of it should be used to wage one critical battle, rather than trying to wage many small battles with limited resources for each. I proposed an all-out assault on adult illiteracy, arguing that literacy would allow those trapped in poverty to take advantage of the economic opportunities we were hoping to make available. My radical suggestion got polite reactions from colleagues but was never taken seriously. Whatever merits it may have had, I soon realized, it was not a realistic idea. The supporters of the other "battles" perceived as critical to the total war effort would never have approved my proposal. The task force was right to work hard to put together a package that was substantively promising but also legislatively possible.

With the constant monitoring by LBJ and his White House aides, the task force did manage to create such a package that was ready for submission by March 16. In an eloquent message to the Congress accompanying the proposed bill, LBJ declared:

> There are millions of Americans—one-fifth of our people—who have not shared in the abundance which has been granted to most of us, and on whom the gates of opportunity have been closed. Most of all [poverty] means hopelessness for the young. . . . The young man or woman who grows up without a decent education, in a broken home, in a hostile and squalid environment, in ill health or in the face of racial injustice—that young man or woman is often trapped in a life of poverty. The war on poverty is not a struggle simply to support people, to make them dependent on the generosity of others. It is a struggle to give people a chance.

Reflecting the sense of urgency that President Johnson had clearly sounded, the House of Representatives started intensive committee hearings on March 17, the very next day. The very title of the bill, "Economic Opportunity Act," had been carefully designed to transmit the central theme. This was no new welfare program; it was an effort to get people out of poverty by giving economic opportunities for self-help. The bill's declaration of purpose then elaborated, in part:

> The United States can achieve its full economic and social potential as a nation only if every individual has the opportunity to contribute to

the full extent of his abilities and to participate in the workings of our society. It is therefore the policy of the United States to eliminate the paradox of poverty in the midst of plenty in this nation by opening to everyone the opportunity for education and training, the opportunity to live in decency and dignity. It is the purpose of these acts to strengthen, supplement, and coordinate efforts in furtherance of that policy.

Despite widespread positive reaction to the proposed legislation, there were the proverbial naysayers who fought every extension of federal responsibility for the general welfare, and there were also responsible critics of some aspects of the draft legislation. LBJ used his considerable parliamentary skills and the prestige of his White House to help secure final agreement between the two houses of Congress on August 8, 1964.

I will never forget that emotion-filled ceremony on August 20 on the South Lawn of the White House when the president signed the bill into law. Hundreds of the nation's leaders from every walk of life felt they were experiencing a great moment in America's social history when they heard the president declare: "For the first time in all the history of the human race, a great nation is able and is willing to make a commitment to eradicate poverty among its people." With that signature, we were to learn, more than a new agency had been launched; more than a few new programs had been authorized. The conscience of the country, its people, its government at every level, and its major organizations had been aroused. None could remain indifferent to the challenge. Other programs not previously labeled "poverty" programs were seen in a new light.

A major illustration of this impact was the campaign to enact health care for older Americans. Since 1949 there had been major efforts to enact what was ultimately to be called Medicare and Medicaid. But year after year, the Congress had been unable to agree to act. But in 1965, in the context of the War on Poverty, there was greater weight attached to provisions for Medicare. While the nonpoor over sixty-five would also be covered, this important health measure would largely serve those over sixty-five who were on limited incomes and faced huge, rising costs. Medicaid was designed specifically for all Americans too poor to afford medical care.

National tax policy is another illustration of the War on Poverty's influence on other programs. Particularly important to our working poor has been the earned income tax credit. Other programs—housing, food stamps, education, manpower training, etc.—have been tailored or expanded to meet the special needs of the poor.

Other chapters in this volume deal with these and other legacies of LBJ's Great Society. These programs all contributed to the escape from poverty by millions of Americans. Certainly, the general health of the economy has been the greatest single explanation for the improved standard of living. But those of us who were involved in implementing the specific programs authorized by the Economic Opportunity Act of 1964 may be permitted to take satisfaction in the fact that every major component in the original package, albeit changed in name in some cases or housed in other agencies, has been continued and substantially expanded over the last thirty-five years. Thus, the legacy has survived eight presidencies and nineteen congressional terms, both Democratic and Republican.

Here is a brief update on a few of the major components of the war on poverty that LBJ signed into law on that memorable August day in the first year of his presidency:

*Community Action*

For thirty-nine years now, despite efforts by hostile administrations to terminate it, community-action programs have continued to serve as the basic local coordinating bodies for a wide range of community-based antipoverty projects. At the millennium, there were over a thousand such bodies in all fifty states. With "maximum feasible participation" by the poor themselves, these bodies bring together the whole spectrum of private and public forces to plan and administer the most promising measures for each particular community. In recent years, Congress has appropriated more than a half-billion dollars for community action.

*Head Start*

Starting in 1965 as an eight-week summer project, this most popular of all anti-poverty programs has helped break the cycle of poverty by providing a comprehensive program that meets the emotional, educational, health, nutritional, and psychological needs of preschool children from low-income families. Now administered by the Department of Health and Human Services, Head Start in 2000 had more than eight hundred thousand children enrolled in all fifty states. Total appropriations had risen from ninety-six million dollars in 1965 to more than five billion for all-day sessions in 2000.

*Job Corps*

A favorite of President Johnson, this program is aimed at reaching youths with the most serious problems and disabilities, the ones least likely to make it into the workforce. Living and working and studying in residential centers, almost two million youngsters have now been provided academic, vocational, and social skills since 1965. In the year 2000, there were over seventy thousand young men and women at numerous centers, at a cost of $1.7 billion, operated by private industry, universities, labor, and local government.

*VISTA*

Described by some as a "domestic Peace Corps" VISTA (Volunteers in Service to America) has attracted thousands of volunteers from local communities and college campuses to help local anti-poverty groups. Later affiliated with President Clinton's Corporation for National Service, the combined service in 2000 had about five thousand volunteers at more than one thousand nonprofit or public agencies.

Other programs either explicitly authorized by the original legislation or stemming from such provisions include the Legal Services Program, Neighborhood Youth Corps, Foster Grandparents, Migrant Labor Service, and Upward Bound. All these programs continue to open up new opportunities for Americans locked in poverty.

How effective has all of this been? When Lyndon Johnson left the White House in 1969, he could and did take satisfaction in the fact that during the five years of his presidency the number of poor Americans had declined by twelve million compared to the thirty-five million at the time he had launched the War on Poverty. But the full meaning of that war went beyond numbers, as he so eloquently wrote a few years after his retirement:

> We started something in motion with the attack on poverty. . . . Poverty became one of the compelling issues of our time. Finally and firmly, it was brought to the conscience of the nation. The poor had finally found their spokesmen. There would be setbacks and frustrations and disappointments ahead. But no one would ever again be able to ignore poverty in our midst.

# Through a Glass Lightly: Reminiscences of the Model Cities Act and LBJ's Dance with Legislation
## Lawrence Levinson

It now reposes in a brown frame, slightly bent and beginning to yellow with age. Through the glass there sits an engraved commemoration to the Great Society, that huge outpouring of the 205 legislative measures that coursed through the decade of the 1960s and forever shaped the values, traditions, and dynamics of American life.

Presented to the president by his last sitting cabinet, signed by names now etched in memories of the times—Rusk and Fowler, Udall and Cohen, Clifford and Freeman, and the rest—that parchment catalogues the "Landmark Laws" of the Lyndon Johnson administration and explains, "with those acts the President and Congress wrote a record of hope and opportunity for America."

In 1963, we see the beginning of the environmental age through the Clean Air Act, in 1964 the Antipoverty and Civil Rights Act, in 1965 Federal Aid to Education, Medicare, and Voting Rights, in 1966 Model Cities and Rent Supplements, over the next two years, Fair Housing, Safe Streets, and Truth in Lending.

One starts that voyage with the sheer scope and breadth of the master control chart that guided the mechanics of legislation. Shaped by LBJ's own passion for fairness and opportunity, and his hopes for a better America, hammered out in countless task force sessions with the best minds in

America, and finally inscribed in the words, commas, and preambles of public law, the Great Society emerged in full form and force.

As a master of the legislative process, LBJ knew every twist and turn, every procedure, every calendar and timetable. For those who worked in the daily, absorbing mission of smelting programmatic thought and concept into the structure of a proposed statute, through the often-labyrinthine passage to enactment, there was but one point of accountability—the president with his "vote counts" sheets, dockets, hearing schedules, proddings, restlessness, demands, and cajoling.

At any point in time, LBJ knew the precise state of his legislative program. "Have Henry Hall Wilson, our distinguished congressional expert, call this House committee chairman to schedule a "hearing first thing." "Why is Muskie holding up Model Cities? Have Califano call him, make a deal, satisfy him. He knows more about poor people than all of you Harvard types. Get Wilbur Cohen to work out the details of my children's health program with Chairman Mills, stop wasting my time, get moving."

One recalls, in a not too dissimilar vein, General George S. Patton, Jr., standing in the Ardennes snow urging his Third Army onto victory by sheer force of command. So it was with LBJ. There was not a minute to spare: "The political pendulum will be swinging against us, it's inevitable that our clout will be ebbing with each passing day. So strike when we can and strike hard." More often than not, the "Potus" (president of the United States) direct line would ring, usually around 4:30 in the afternoon, that constant, steady ring, no beeps, no stops. Refreshed from his daily pajama-clad nap, the president spoke with that slow drawl, fairly calm but always with an air of menacing impatience, usually provoked to challenge, "Do I need to call Dirksen, should I bring Long and Mansfield over, where are Boggs and McCormick on this, is Albert holding up the Rules Committee? Have O'Brien at his office tomorrow morning!"

And so it went. Day after day, when congressional inertia slowed down a favored LBJ proposal, like rent supplements for the poor, or when tax bills threatened to snarl civil rights legislation, the president was on the front lines, twisting Republican arms if need be, working out compromises with the leadership, fine-tuning proposals sometimes submitted in haste, taking his own personal measure of who was strong and who was weak, calling on support from the business world ("Have Henry Ford contact the Michigan delegation!") or the legal profession ("Get Cutler to call his client Henry Kaiser—I need votes from the Californians!").

Defining moments arrived—but for LBJ, not all too soon—at bill-signing ceremonies. With pen in one hand, giving congratulatory handshakes with the other, he spoke in a strong voice to an attentive audience and a background of congressmen who wanted to make their presences known behind the signing table. Each stroke of the presidential pen metered out a step forward toward a more just and open nation.

To illustrate the gates and hurdles of the legislative process, I have selected the Model Cities Act, one of LBJ's stirring victories in the Eighty-Ninth Congress. This discussion focuses on the prototypical cycle of how a presidential program progressed from its incubation stage, by way of highly disciplined and committed task forces, to the drafting by the agency involved and the White House staff of a concrete piece of legislation. From that point, it was handed off under the watchful gaze of LBJ to the congressional affairs branch of the department, reinforced by the White House, and then onto a full-court press that moved legislation through Congress. At the end of the process, in most cases, emerged a public law, its enactment commemorated, more often than not, by the president in a signing ceremony. Thus the legislative ritual ran its course, and it was then up to the agency to carry out the mandate of law.

Model Cities is key to the understanding of the "dance of legislation." The two primary actors during the Model Cities conceptual stage—Professors Bob Wood of MIT and Charles Haar of Harvard Law School—were, in the words of LBJ, "promoted from armchair generals to frontline commanders" to running the program at HUD, the cabinet department newly created under the president's plan to modernize the federal government.

Perhaps no other Great Society initiative better symbolized LBJ's energetic and thoughtful approach to solving the problems of urban America than the Model Cities program. Developed by the best minds available in the business, labor, and academic communities, it was first set forth in a passionate presidential message on January 26, 1966, on the plight and fate of the American city, and then fought through a year of bitter congressional debate. The Model Cities program emerged scarred but safe. Today it is seen as a bold but unfulfilled experiment in eradicating urban blight and in focusing city renewal not only on "bricks and mortar" but on an array of coordinated social and economic services, designed to lift poor communities out of squalor and into hope.

Model Cities did not start out so named. As it evolved from the presidential task force that gave it form and substance, the program was titled

"Demonstration Cities." The shapers of the concept wanted to depart from the conventional inner-city revitalization approach and undertake "on the job," if you will, an experiment in which new methods, new funding sources, and new ways to coordinate an array of targeted services would be tried out, revised, and ultimately delivered. The task force thinkers included Walter Reuther (then the president of the United Auto Workers), Charles Haar, Dr. Wood, and Whitney Young of the National Urban League. All of the task force members were given this mandate by LBJ: "Forget the politics, it's *my* job, but give me the freshest and most creative ideas you can come up with."

To add the experience of the American business community, the task force relied on the advice and good practical sense of Ben Heineman, chairman of the Chicago and Northwestern Railroad, and Edgar Kaiser, chairman of Kaiser Industries. To design a structure for the legislation, the task force drew upon the knowledge and background of two of the nation's most distinguished metropolitan experts: William Rafsky of the Philadelphia Urban Renewal Agency and Professor Chester Rapkin of the University of Pennsylvania, who headed the support staff of technical experts. Because the president placed enormous importance on the work of the Model Cities Task Force, he assigned White House Counsel Harry McPherson to provide insight and continuity. McPherson was later to play a major role in clearing the legislation through a restless and fractious Congress. To add congressional flavor to the work of the task force, the president asked Connecticut senator Abe Ribicoff to join in its deliberations—a wise move since the senator, months later, along with Senator Ed Muskie of Maine, became one of the saviors of the program.

As the task force began its work in early 1965, the nation was gripped by a conviction that the crisis of the central city had to be attacked with vigor and imagination. To capitalize upon that spirit, President Johnson sought to launch a bold new program to revitalize the slums that were the shame of a modern nation. As one who understood the failures of the traditional urban-renewal programs, the breakdown of order and civility in inadequate and dilapidated government-sponsored public housing, LBJ was determined to set American out on a new road to recovery. As reflected in his January 1966 speech on Model Cities, "We must set in motion the forces of change in great urban areas that will make them the masterpieces of our civilization" and in "an effort larger in scope, more comprehensive, more concentrated than any that has gone before."

While the rhetoric today seems grandiose, it nonetheless embodied a determination to alter the status quo and strike out in new directions. All of this happened at a time when Watts had just burned (let us not "reward the rioters" was the watchword of the day), when Vietnam was beginning to intrude into the American conscience, when budget crunchers had sent out signals about "no new programs," and when the landmark 1964 and 1965 civil rights legislation had just become law. The nation was trying to adjust, not always peacefully, to these dramatic changes. Issues of race, funding, bureaucratic infighting and inertia, congressional resistance, and the ebbing of presidential power all came into play as the Model Cities legislation was being shaped. Undeterred by these obstacles, the president and his task force moved forward with enthusiasm and with dedication.

In early 1965, President Johnson was deeply impressed by a presentation by Walter Reuther, an epic figure in American labor history who now argued that decaying urban cities could survive only if an array, or cross section, of social and economic services were introduced into a few selected poorest neighborhoods as a demonstration project, that ultimately an "urban TVA" was needed to reverse the decline of the American metropolis. LBJ grasped the sheer force of Reuther's idea. Shortly after I joined the White House staff, in July 1965, a task force organized to build on the Reuther concept was in full swing. The group labored throughout the last five months of 1965, hammering into shape the measure that would become the centerpiece of the president's 1966 legislative agenda. In mid-December 1965, just before the State of the Union message, the report of the task force, shrouded by secrecy, was submitted to the president. Joe Califano briefed LBJ on the proposal. The president gave him the "green light to charge forward," warning against any press leaks (except those that he felt he had to make himself)—he wanted to surprise the nation with his new, far reaching legislative initiative. Indeed, the president hinted as much in his State of the Union Address, when he promised to deliver "a program to rebuild completely, on a scale never before attempted, entire central and slum areas of our cities."

Thus the gauntlet was laid down, and the stormy passage from a speech to a public law began in earnest. It took just a little short of a year for the transformation of a programmatic proposal into a public law. On November 3, 1966, with the stroke of his signing pen, a proud president made the "Demonstration Cities and Metropolitan Development Act" the law of the land.

What was this proposal that created so much controversy in Congress and even within the newly formed HUD? Was it an idea ahead of its time? Could "Demonstration Cities" effectively work at the city level? Could it reverse the rapid cycle of urban decay that posed one of the most formidable challenges to policy makers at all levels of government?

The Model Cities program had three central components that set it apart from all urban legislation that preceded it. First, it required the close federal coordination of a series of targeted neighborhood-revitalization efforts in health, job creation, housing, education, and social services, using a mix of federal and state funding. Second, it placed a premium on local initiative, by offering special planning grants to encourage local agencies to develop model-city approaches. Third, it created incentives through special block (or supplementary) federal grants to develop novel and untried but potentially workable comprehensive solutions to counter inner-city blight. The heart of the task force's approach was to deploy these grants quickly into selected cities (no more than sixty) and show Congress that positive results could be achieved in these "demonstration areas." This would set the stage for more funding.

From the White House staff's perspective, the task-force approach had political drawbacks that had to be carefully assessed. For example, why would Congress vote funds for a program "not in my backyard"? Would mayors, jealous of their turf prerogatives, yield the program's control to a federal coordinator? Was the message of racial integration too starkly portrayed as a major program direction, particularly after the race riots that had torn into American cities after Watts? Would the private sector respond by hitherto "red lined" investments in slum neighborhoods?

The president thoughtfully mulled these issues over, thinking that Congress in any event would transform and confront these issues as the measure progressed through the Housing and Banking Committees. But there was no time to lose. On the evening before the bill was sent to Congress, we unwrapped the secret Model Cities package and explained to an awed congressional audience in the White House basement the scope and depth of the measure. It would require $2.3 billion in new money over six years, applied to sixty cities, and would involve twelve million dollars in local planning grants.

LBJ had urged us to "speed things up and get the bill introduced "real fast." "Get Patman [fellow Texan and chairman of the House Banking and Currency Committee] and Douglas [chairman of the counterpart

Senate Committee] and sign up as many sponsors as they can get hold of to start hearings. We will have to first go to the House, then the Senate, because the Senate will be reluctant to move first."

For the next ten months, the measure floundered, almost died, and came back to life. Were it not for the personal intervention of the president with Senator Ed Muskie of Maine, the bill would have been seen as an example of presidential failure, dropped into the scrap heap of measures that died in committee.

Senator Muskie, later to run for the presidency, later yet to become Jimmy Carter's secretary of state, found himself in the White House one spring day in the midst of the legislative crisis that threatened to derail the bill. Because of congressional inaction, controversy, and conflict, a leadership vacuum had emerged. To propel the legislation forward, to resurrect it from the pile of passed over measures, new leadership was essential. LBJ knew as much. The fate of the program hung by a thread until extra presidential force and persuasion could be applied.

Muskie, a Senate leader in the environmental field, was sufficiently impressed by LBJ to offer to take up the leadership role. Joe Califano was sent to brief the senator the next day and then flew up to Maine to meet with him over a reportedly excellent lobster stew lunch. I was then delegated to work out the senator's concerns with his capable legislative assistant, Dan Nicoll, over morning coffee in the second-floor White House conference room. After much tugging and pulling, refining of language, and exchanges of drafts, and largely through the efforts of Senators Muskie and Ribicoff, the bill's shape finally emerged. Instead of $2.3 billion over six years, the compromise was $900 million over two years. Instead of limiting the grants to the sixty or so large cities, small and medium cities were declared eligible also, as were rural areas, to attract more congressional support. A concept of a federal "czar" was dropped, but an additional twelve million dollars in planning grants was added to the second year to allow cities who failed the first time to qualify for a second chance.

Muskie, a strong proponent of metropolitan planning, added a new section to stimulate the role of metropolitan agencies. He insisted that the supplemental grants, where the big money was, not be used for general city expenses, such as mayors' salaries, but had to be confined to supporting innovative programs in the targeted slum neighborhoods.

The seminal moment in the course of the legislative struggle was the direct and personal intervention of LBJ. Having successfully persuaded

Muskie to take the lead, the president turned his attention to the public. In early October, in a widely covered press conference, LBJ urged the passage of the bill: "As I said in the beginning, and as I would repeat again, I think it [Model Cities] is one of the most important pieces of legislation for the good of all Americans . . . that we can act upon this session."

With this "fall offensive" impetus, the bill gathered legislative speed. In meetings with the president, Joe Califano and I were urged to "get cracking" and get business tycoons "who are our friends" to weigh in, "get Meany [George Meany, powerful head of the AFL-CIO] to weigh in, and don't forget the homebuilders who need our help." In advertisements and op-ed pieces in the nation's press, a private-sector coalition headed by Henry Ford and David Rockefeller called upon the House to pass promptly the Model Cities bill as an "imaginative response" to the problems of the American community.

All of this was orchestrated by LBJ, who had his finger on the pulse and rhythm of the congressional process, from the intricacies of the House Rules Committee, to "discharge petitions," to the personalities of the committee chairmen, to the movement of legislation on "suspense" or "unanimous consent" calendars. These were the tools in the hands of a master legislative craftsman, who could achieve results by beating the odds, who knew all too well the sometimes mysterious ways in which Congress worked, and how the power of persuasion could reverse the tide of defeat and lead to victory. Despite the doubters and naysayers, the measure emerged, bruised but safe. In late October, the House vote was a narrow 142-126; the Senate vote was 38–22. On November 3, 1966, the president signed the measure. The term Demonstration Cities" was no longer in vogue, since it conjured up memories of the cities scarred by the race riots of 1965 and 1966. The more descriptive title of "Model Cities" was adopted in its place.

As a postscript, the Model Cities Administration was established at HUD under the capable leadership of Assistant Secretary Ralph Taylor. In the first wave of grants, sixty-three cities were awarded planning funds during November 1966, after the midterm elections. Every city with a population of over one million was included, except for Los Angeles—then headed by Mayor Sam Yorty, who was considered ill equipped to administer the program. Two midsized cities were included, as were eight small towns. In March 1967, twelve more cities were added. Just before LBJ left office, nine cities across the nation received full funding for their programs, as described in their planning-grant applications. From Atlanta to Waco, from Boston to Huntsville, Model Cities, characterized by innovative approaches that captured the spirit of the new law, got off to a successful start.

Consider Boston, for example. Programs of citizen education, neighborhood development, family health centers, drug addiction rehabilitation, employment and manpower counseling, welfare assistance, adult education, education for the mentally retarded, child care, police-community relations, and parks and recreation were all targeted for the slums. It was an example of how the Model Cities approach could be applied to solve problems across a wide spectrum of inner-city needs.

But soon all this was to come to an unhappy end. The Nixon administration's aversion to Great Society programs, the fact that many cities were run by Democratic mayors, and budget and philosophical differences committed the program to a slow dance to oblivion. Because of the gaps between authorization, funding, and program delivery, and the years it takes to carry out a high-intensity complex program like Model Cities, the clock simply ran out.

Be that as it may, Model Cities stands as a tribute to a caring president who seized a small window of opportunity to attack the problems of, as Lincoln Steffens wrote at the turn of the twentieth century, the "Shame of the Cities." Model Cities opened up a robust debate on the future of American neighborhoods and the role of federal government in partnership with local communities to solve the problems of urban decline. Model Cities eventually led to a new form of block-grant revenue sharing and a recognition that modern housing, while crucial, was not enough. More needed to be done, in the form of a broad range of safety-net programs, including, as it turned out, Head Start, job training, children's health—those "Great Society" programs that continue to flourish today with renewed support and funding. As we look back over the past three decades, Model Cities stands as a proud moment in the history of "can-do" presidency. To improve the quality of urban life, LBJ offered a vision best expressed in the form of a question as relevant today as it was first posed in January 1966: "Shall we make our cities livable for ourselves and our posterity or shall we by timidity and neglect doom to fester and decay?" It is not too late to begin again.

More than three decades later, that catalogue of LBJ's "Landmark Laws" hangs on the wall of my study, a memory of the past that still echoes today in the way Americans see themselves. As the president was often moved to say, "I had lived thoroughly every hour of those past five years. I had known sorrow and anger, frustration and disappointment, pain and dismay. But more than anything else, I had experienced a towering pride and pleasure at having my chance to make my contribution to solving the problems of our times." Those of us who were fortunate enough to have been part of that journey would never have thrown a minute of it away, for we all shared that "towering pride."

# Vietnam: Lyndon Johnson's Choice
## *Peter R. Rosenblatt*

The war in Vietnam has been the single most divisive event in American history since the Civil War. It loomed over Lyndon Johnson's five-year presidency, inhibiting today a full appreciation of his achievements, which were perhaps more significant than those of any comparable period in more than a century.

The emotions generated by the war have also obscured the war's own place in history. The enormous weight of conventional wisdom, settling into near consensus—that the war was a tragic mistake, that it was fought over a region of no strategic significance to the United States, that it ended in military defeat and was in any event unwinnable—silenced and in some cases convinced many of those who at the time held contrary views.

It is essential to an understanding of President Johnson's decisions on the war that they be considered in the context of their time, including, most significantly, the major objectives of his administration, the contemporaneous Washington perspective on the Cold War and the politics of the debate over withdrawal versus escalation. Only then can one begin to grasp fully the impossibility of the choices with which the new president was confronted from his first day in office.

Lyndon Johnson's priorities, from his first race for a House seat in rural Texas to his elevation to the presidency, *always* focused on domestic policy, specifically on improving the lives and opening opportunities for those who had been bypassed as America evolved into an ever more prosperous and just society. As a marginalized vice president, he watched in silent frustration as the Kennedy administration permitted its modest reform agenda to languish in Congress.

As president he did not at first fully realize the extent to which the rapidly deteriorating Southeast Asian conflict would threaten his domestic priorities. He strove to hold the war in check while he focused his energies on transforming America, but he soon came to realize that *any* decision he made on Vietnam would jeopardize and possibly destroy his ability to achieve all of his domestic goals. He dealt with the dilemma by making war decisions on what he considered necessary political, military, and diplomatic grounds alone, relying on his immense political skills to preserve as much as possible of the War on Poverty and his other priorities.

Johnson's foreign policy views were in close accord with those of the Kennedy administration. These, in turn, represented a continuum from the bipartisan accord of which Johnson had been a principal architect as Senate majority leader during the Eisenhower administration. This accord viewed the United States as the bulwark against an increasingly powerful, self-confident world communist threat led by the Soviet Union, supported by China, and single-mindedly focused on global dominance by means of persuasion, subversion, and the threat or use of force wherever and whenever an opportunity presented itself. "Wars of national liberation," in particular, had become a favored Soviet vehicle in the Third World. Reports of a Sino-Soviet split were widely discounted as the speculation of scholars, since both countries seemed to pursue similar anti-Western courses, whether or not the result of coordination. Both needed to be "contained" by the West, with the United States at the forefront. In the early 1960s it was sometimes difficult to tell where Soviet involvement in subversion ended and the Chinese began.

The bipartisanship in foreign policy that obtained when Johnson became president had been built slowly on a series of Cold War events during the previous two decades. Beginning with the forcible Soviet imposition of communist dictatorships in Eastern and Central Europe and continuing with the Greek and Chinese civil wars, the Berlin blockade, the Korean War, the Malayan insurgency, the Chinese threat to Taiwan, the French Indochina War, the Hungarian uprising, communist subversion in Iran, Guatemala, the Middle East, Africa and elsewhere, and the communist takeover of Cuba, communist forces seemed to be on the offensive in every quarter of the world. This impression was heightened following the Kennedy administration's disastrous attempt at a counterstroke at the Bay of Pigs, a hundred miles from Florida; by the subsequent Cuban missile crisis; and by the Berlin crisis, which necessitated a partial mobilization of U.S. military reserves. The insurgencies sponsored by North Vietnam against South Vietnam and the nearby "domino" of Laos fit neatly into a bipartisan consensus view of a world in which Russian and Chinese-supported communists were gaining ground against the West through the use or threat of force, externally supported revolution, and subversion. The West was on the defensive. The Cold War was considered a zero-sum game, in which every gain of one side was a loss to the other. Kennedy's election victory was in some measure based upon his exaggerated warnings that Soviet progress in space technology had created a "missile gap" in their favor. Whether or not Kennedy believed this to be true, it was believed by many and supported the widespread sentiment that resistance to any and all further efforts at expansion by the communist powers was essential.

Lurking behind this bipartisan accord on the communist threat, however, was the recollection among most Democrats that many Republicans still in leadership positions had, only a decade earlier, accused them of being "soft on communism"—a charge that coexisted uneasily with a second charge, that a Democratic president had presided over the initiation of each of the nation's twentieth-century wars. These charges had given birth to the McCarthyite fury, which had created a political imperative for any Democratic president or aspirant to avoid seeming less than tough on international proponents of communism (a principle that Democrats abandoned, to their cost, from the end of the Johnson administration to the end of the Cold War). Moreover, the uncertainties of the election year 1964, already rife with rumors that the Kennedy assassination might have been sponsored by the Soviets or the Cubans, were exacerbated by the indisputable fact that Lyndon Johnson had inherited the presidency as the result of an assassination that had occurred in his own state.

When Johnson became president, Kennedy's domestic legislative legacy hung in the balance. Johnson pulled it out of the fire and initiated an unprecedented legislative program of his own. He coped decisively and effectively with the foreign policy transition issues, but he came to understand that there were no satisfactory alternatives on Vietnam.

South Vietnam was in chaos. A drastically deteriorating political situation and near military collapse had induced a reluctant President Kennedy to give his consent to a military coup against President Ngo Dinh Diem, a coup that unexpectedly resulted in the deaths of Diem and his powerful brother just three weeks before Kennedy's own assassination. The U.S. commitment to, and military presence in, that unfortunate country and its smaller neighbor, Laos, had increased incrementally, particularly under Kennedy, as South Vietnam weakened. By November 21, 1963, 16,000 American troops had been committed there. Not long after inheriting the presidency Johnson was told that this number of troops was insufficient to stabilize the now leaderless country.

There can be no doubt that if Johnson had faced a clean slate in Vietnam he would not have sent the 16,000 troops he found there or made any major troop commitment. But far from facing a clean slate, he found that substantial, actual, and tacit commitments had been made by his predecessors that narrowed his options to only a few alternatives, none of which was either satisfactory or promising. The announcement of a U.S. withdrawal, with or without an agreement with North Vietnam, would have resulted in the rapid collapse of the shaky post-Diem government of South Vietnam (the GVN) and of resistance to the communists in Laos and neutral Cambodia. The prevalent "domino" theory held that the fall of the three Indochinese states would place all of the newly independent nations of Southeast Asia at risk.

While withdrawal was certainly an option for a new administration not fully responsible for the commitments of its predecessors, such action would have found few supporters in either political party. It would have laid the president open to charges of "softness on communism" and desertion of an ally. These charges would, the president knew, be made not only by the Republicans, whose national convention was soon to nominate "Mr. Conservative," Senator Barry Goldwater, for the presidency but by Kennedy loyalists, whose martyred leader had intensified the U.S. obligation to Vietnam by a troop buildup and by his support for the coup against the murdered Diem. The president's conviction was widely shared, furthermore, that withdrawal would diminish U.S. credibility worldwide, undermine the faith that allies and many of the nonaligned nations placed in American support, and feed a global perception that communism was the wave of the future.

Thus, President Johnson's decisions on Vietnam were not made in the perfect vacuum that is now so often postulated. It was not a question of whether or not to intervene; rather, the issue was whether or not to withdraw from an intervention that had already occurred and, if the intervention was to be sustained, how to prevent collapse of the Western position there without igniting a nuclear war. Withdrawal under fire, leaving a dependent ally to be overrun by an insurgency directed from Hanoi and supported and supplied by China and the Soviet Union, would raise profound foreign policy and political issues that extended far beyond the scene of battle. Johnson also knew that withdrawal would collapse the bipartisan foreign policy consensus while also depriving him of Republican support that was essential to his plans for domestic reform, that included civil rights and other legislation opposed by southern Democrats.

If the president was unwilling to accept the choice of withdrawal, he was not, on the other hand, prepared to acquiesce in the counsel of some of his national security advisers that he risk widening the war by an abrupt and dramatic escalation. He was acutely aware that a previous escalation of that character, MacArthur's thrust toward the North Korean border with China, had precipitated Chinese intervention a decade and a half earlier. The president knew that major escalation would, furthermore, have produced little support and, probably, major opposition from U.S. allies even as it weakened the already divided Democratic congressional support for his domestic programs.

President Johnson's strategy for dealing with Vietnam was founded on the perception that he must pursue a middle course between abandonment of the field in the face of the enemy and unrestricted use of the full power of the United States against North Vietnam. He therefore decided on an initial, measured increase of several thousand U.S. troops. He hoped these would suffice to contain the situation until a stable new post-Diem GVN could mobilize South Vietnamese resistance. The president strongly suspected that this represented, in Samuel Johnson's words, the triumph of hope over experience. He also knew that all of the alternatives were worse, and he placed such hopes as he had in the assessments of his military advisers. But whether or not these proved reliable, he knew that in this case, just as in the case of his civil rights legislation, it had to be done; he believed it right, and there were no bet-ter alternatives.

As the Vietnam crisis intensified in 1964, Johnson remained con-vinced that reaction from the political right to any sign of administration weakness or retreat represented a far greater political threat than the left's growing opposition to involvement in the war. He felt that the views of the right commanded potential majority support in the country and that U.S. withdrawal from Vietnam would play directly into its hands, threat-ening his global foreign policy of resisting communism by means short of war with China and the Soviet Union, as well as his plans for major do-mestic reform. He was convinced that adopting the prescriptions of the right could invite Chinese or Soviet intervention to save North Vietnam from collapse, possibly even precipitating a nuclear war. Thus, while all-out war in Indochina would risk a nuclear confrontation, withdrawal could elect Goldwater president in 1964 and ultimately produce all-out war in any event. The political left could not impose its views on Viet-nam as long as he was president, but the right had a base in the Republi-can party with which he could deal but that, in the last analysis, he could not control.

The political pressures on Johnson after his landslide 1964 reelection were temporarily diminished, but they were by no means eliminated. By this time, one year into Johnson's presidency, his middle-way policy of in-creasing the American commitment in Vietnam only to the extent nec-essary to stave off GVN collapse had brought U.S. troop levels to some 20,000 and had further committed the country to the war.

The president sought the Gulf of Tonkin Resolution of August 1964 largely to preserve presidential control over a rapidly fluctuating situa-tion, not as a blank check for preplanned major escalation as is so often charged. Johnson continued to pursue his middle course. He resisted the counsel of many of his advisers for immediate entry into major ground and air combat, even as he rejected the pleas of others for a pullout. Knowing all the while that he had *no good* options, he had to agree to ad-ditional troops (though rarely as many as the military requested), more air strikes, assistance to the South Vietnamese army (the ARVN), aid for counterinsurgency programs, and more economic support.

He was perfectly aware that Vietnam and China were traditional ene-mies, but he also knew that North Vietnam could not sustain its war effort without the massive support it was daily receiving from China, Russia, and other members of the communist bloc. He knew that the Soviet Union had demonstrated its readiness to use force rather than permit the fall of communist governments in East Germany in 1953 and Hungary in 1956. China had gone to war with the United States to prevent the fall of a communist government in North Korea in 1951. The conventional wisdom of the time was that while all noncommunist governments were subject to communist subversion and that such efforts had to be thwarted locally by conventional political or military measures, the major communist powers would risk a nuclear war before permitting an existing communist government to fall. The president felt that the only way the situation in South Vietnam could be dealt with without courting another major war with China, or even World War III, was by defeating the Viet Cong and the North Vietnamese army (NVA) through the use of land forces in the South, supplemented by air power in both Vietnams.

President Johnson was not optimistic that this approach, sustained every few months by further troop commitments, would produce victory, though he was quite confident that it would prevent defeat. But he remained convinced that each of the other choices was worse. He gave the middle way everything he had, even as he worked miracles in his domestic legislative program. He did not believe that pounding from the air and by the half-million U.S. troops on the ground in the South would break the North's morale. But he had participated in the war against a no less determined Japanese enemy, which had, in the end, given up when it had run out of military options. Determination was not everything; Johnson continued to hope that military pressure would persuade the leaders of North Vietnam that victory was beyond their reach and that the kind of compromise settlement that had never been offered the Japanese was their best political alternative.

Here we come to the heart of the matter. During the course of the 1965–1968 buildup, the president was buying time for General William Westmoreland's and the Joint Chiefs of Staff's strategy of attrition through large-unit "search and destroy" operations. He had little confidence in forecasts that this strategy alone would produce victory—he insisted on upgrading both the counterinsurgency effort against the Viet Cong and aid to the GVN—but he hoped that it would produce sufficient battlefield and GVN political stability to bring about at least a Korea-type stalemate. That, in turn, could pave the way for a U.S. exit under honorable circumstances even if the North remained unresponsive to his repeated negotiating overtures. Such an outcome, leaving both Vietnams, like both Koreas, intact, would avoid the terrible alternatives of a wider war and the perception of U.S. abandonment of an ally, thus limiting damage to American global interests. It would permit the president once more to give his undivided attention to his domestic legislative agenda. His legislative program needed time. Johnson had been a participant in the New and Fair Deals, which had taken twenty years. He could not have known when he became president in 1963 that he would have only five years in which to legislate comparable achievements.

Stated otherwise, President Johnson felt that he could make the decisions required of him by the war situation while still pursuing his domestic goals, but he understood that his ability to achieve all of the latter hung, in great measure, on the success of the former.

If by mid-1967 Johnson's middle way had not yet stabilized Vietnam, it had begun, despite mounting opposition to the war at home, to establish a certain military equilibrium. At least, the North Vietnamese command had been persuaded that the prospect of victory through its own costly counterstrategy of attrition was receding. The NVA therefore embarked on a radical shift in strategy, involving a simultaneous nationwide offensive against the cities of the South. It would employ literally all of the NVA's and Viet Cong's assets in a single, all-or-nothing effort to knock the GVN out of the war and thereby force U.S. withdrawal.

In the early morning hours of January 31, 1968, in the midst of a Buddhist New Year (Tet) truce, the NVA launched what was to become the most important battle of the war, the so-called Tet offensive. In thus reversing its strategy the enemy abandoned an approach that had maximized its battlefield advantages for one that shifted the advantage to U.S. forces, with their vastly superior mobility and firepower. The fighting was hard and costly, but the ultimate outcome was unambiguous in military terms. The NVA was badly mauled, and the Viet Cong's clandestine cells were exposed and all but destroyed, never to arise again as a serious nationwide threat.

The tragic ironies of this decisive event boggle the mind; the North Vietnamese took the huge gamble of reversing their strategy on the basis of a complete misunderstanding of the political temper of South Vietnam. They had assumed that a simultaneous Viet Cong rising and NVA invasion of the cities of the South would be met with open arms, rather than fierce resistance. They suffered a crushing military and political defeat where they expected to win, in South Vietnam, yet they won a vic-tory in the United States, due to an antiwar reaction that, in their lack of experience, they had failed to foresee. In our country a battle that, in military terms, could have proved as decisive a victory as Midway became instead a byword for disappointed hopes.

The negotiations with North Vietnam that followed President John-son's announcement two months after Tet that he would not seek reelec-tion began a process that, in 1973, achieved a solution very much like the one that President Johnson had sought—an honorable U.S. exit and turnover of the war to a stable GVN supported by a more competent and better-equipped ARVN.

Some part of the responsibility for the war's ultimate outcome two years later must be borne by the Nixon administration, which skillfully negotiated and managed the U.S. withdrawal while supporting the GVN, and by the GVN itself, which, with all its manifest failings, nonetheless fought on quite alone for those two years. Far greater responsibility, how-ever, must be borne by the U.S. Congress, which cut off the army and people of South Vietnam from outside support in the face of an enemy massively supported by allies. That, in the end, broke South Vietnam's will to resist, which we had nurtured at such fearful cost.

Why, one might ask, was the honorable-withdrawal scenario achieved by President Nixon four years later not attainable during the presidency of Lyndon Johnson, when that was the outcome that he, himself, had sought? I think there are two principal reasons.

Firstly, South Vietnam was close to military and political collapse when Johnson inherited the war on November 21, 1963. The events of from 1963 to 1968—the U.S. military buildup and battlefield successes, the destruction of the Viet Cong as a major military force, achievement of some degree of GVN political stability under President Nguyen Thieu and Prime Minister Nguyen Cao Ky, the bolstering of ARVN main-force units, the implementation of an aggressive counterinsurgency program, and major aid to the GVN—all laid the groundwork for the conditions that, under the Nixon administration's skillful management, permitted an honorable U.S. withdrawal four years later.

The second reason was the fact that General Creighton Abrams suc-ceeded to the command of the Military Assistance Command, Vietnam, only after the Tet offensive, in the waning months of the Johnson ad-ministration. General Abrams has recently begun to come into his own as a pivotal figure as his accomplishments have become more widely understood. His predecessor, Westmoreland, and the Joint Chiefs pursued a strategy that had proven successful in our two previous wars—use of large, powerful units to find and fix enemy forces and destroy them wherever they might be, in preference to clearing territory and defending populations. ARVN units were generally denigrated and used only as auxiliaries. Poorly trained, equipped, and motivated, Vietnamese local and regional forces were usually unable or unwilling to carry out their assigned task of dealing with the Viet Cong, giving the latter a free run of the countryside. The strategy that sought to grind down the NVA by inflicting sustained levels of casualties presumed to be unacceptable played, instead, directly to the NVA's strength—its ability to avoid decisive, war-ending defeats by slipping away across borders or into jungles that U.S. forces could not readily traverse, and to replace its heavy casualties from a seemingly inexhaustible pool of northern recruits. The attrition strategy might, in the end, have worked, but at a human cost that the American public was unwilling to pay.

The Abrams strategy, on the other hand, shifted the emphasis from large-unit sweeps toward clearing the enemy from the population centers through combined U.S.-ARVN main-force and counterinsurgency actions, and it accorded ever greater responsibility and authority to the ARVN. Continued as Nixon's policy of "Vietnamization," it achieved significant progress within two years.

President Johnson was no military strategist himself. He was supremely confident of his personal judgment in domestic affairs, but he felt compelled to seek the best advice available to him on how to employ America's tremendous ground and air power against the NVA wisely. Nonetheless, he did not supinely accept the Joint Chiefs's ceaseless requests for more troops with which to pursue a flawed strategy. But it was only under General Abrams, after the NVA suffered its staggering military defeat at Tet, that the military situation began to stabilize. By then the Johnson administration was in its final months.

President Johnson's fear that the war issue would play into the hands of his adversaries on the right rather than to those on the left was ultimately borne out by the election of Richard Nixon—for most Democrats, the arch right-winger—in 1968. What Johnson did not foresee was that Nixon would turn out to be a highly skilled successor, able both to contain the Republican right and to build on the military and diplomatic initiatives that Johnson had mounted in the final year of his presidency.

The historical significance of the war will probably not be clearly understood for some time. One thing, however, does seem certain—it will be viewed less as a free-standing war than as one in a long series of battles in the forty-four-year Cold War. In this context Vietnam takes its place alongside the Berlin airlift, the Korean War, the Hungarian rebellion, the Cuban missile crisis, the Prague Spring of 1968, the Soviet war in Afghanistan, and countless less well-remembered episodes in which the armed forces of one or another of the two major antagonists became involved in potentially cataclysmic encounters somewhere on the globe. The ultimate outcome of the Cold War was, of course, an unambiguous and total victory for the West, but the causes of the victory remain the subject of debate on both sides of the former divide. History provides no other example of a major power collapsing without the proximate cause of military defeat, utter economic ruin, or internal revolt. It will therefore be necessary for future Cold War historians, unaffected by the emotions that the Vietnam War still arouses, to determine what role each of the Cold War's major events—of which Vietnam was unquestionably one of the most important—played in its ultimate outcome.

I suspect that such future analyses will continue a recent tendency toward the view that while the fall of Saigon in 1975 may have seemed to signal the victory of North Vietnam, the fall of the Berlin Wall a quarter-century later may have been influenced by President Johnson's courageous determination neither to walk away from that fight nor permit it to spin out of control into a world war, though it might have cost him the completion of his domestic agenda and the continuation of his presidency.

# SECTION SIX

# The Best We Ever Had: Johnson and Civil Rights

Bayard Rustin, a leading theorist in the civil rights movement, remarked that the Johnson administration and President Johnson were the "best we've ever had" with regard to their contributions to civil rights. In many respects the Johnson years were a watershed in the struggle for racial equality in the United States, yet problems remain. Nicholas Deb Katzenbach and Lee White examine Johnson's civil rights activities. Their essays answer questions and raise others. What were the president's and his staff's motives for promoting civil rights? Was he able to walk effectively the middle ground between white conservatives and black militants? What impact did the Vietnam War have on civil rights? How skillfully and imaginatively did Johnson and his staff operate within existing political institutions to foster civil rights? In other words, how far was the president willing to move to challenge the vestiges of racial equality? Should, or could, he have done more? Did the president personally pay close attention to the vital details of the bureaucratic operations involved in civil rights, or did he distance himself from the day-to-day operations of those programs? Did his solutions promote genuine equality of opportunity? Can Johnson's approach to solving racial problems—by a redistribution of economic and political power—work? Can we today devise federal remedies to cure racial ills? How would Johnson today view the attacks on affirmative action? How would he view quotas for hiring?

# Toward a More Just America for All: Johnson the Civil Rights Warrior
## Nicholas deBelleville Katzenbach

When Lyndon Johnson took the presidential oath on that fateful November day, there was no way of knowing for certain that his priorities would be different from those of President Kennedy. A sitting vice president, at least one as loyal to JFK as Johnson had been, supports his administration, repressing whatever policy differences he may have with the president.

Those of us in Robert Kennedy's Justice Department were most anxious about LBJ's views on civil rights—an anxiety shared by civil rights leaders, most liberals, and much of the public. Would this new president from the South carry on with Kennedy's recent initiatives or merely give them lip service? Would his support for the civil rights legislation be vigorous and effective?

There were reasons to be concerned. While LBJ as Senate majority leader had successfully promoted in 1957 and 1960 enactment of the first civil rights legislation since the post–Civil War acts, that legislation was more symbolic than real. To avoid a filibuster, compromises had had to be made that watered that legislation down to the point of relative ineffectiveness. Would the legislation recently introduced by President Kennedy suffer the same fate? Further, as president of the Senate, Vice President Johnson had declined in 1961 to support a liberal effort to reduce the rule, the vote required, to limit debate (that is, to end a filibuster) from sixty-seven votes to sixty.

There were also reasons to be encouraged. It was LBJ who had been responsible in early 1961 for the executive order on nondiscriminatory employment by government contractors. I had been involved in that order, with Bill Moyers and Hobart Taylor—and my role had been mostly to modify strong provisions that I thought went beyond the power of the executive acting without Congress. Although limited in its scope, the order was effective in securing black employment and use of minority-owned businesses by government contractors. Hobart Taylor had coined the phrase "affirmative action," and the idea of government helping blacks to overcome racial discrimination began to catch on. Similarly, the then–vice president had insisted on a fair-employment provision in the draft of civil rights legislation recently submitted to the Congress by JFK—a provision we all agreed was desirable but one we feared would go beyond what the House, let alone the Senate, would accept. Similarly, LBJ had made a number of civil rights speeches as vice president strongly supporting the views of civil rights leaders. Had they been rhetoric to support the administration and the Democratic platform, or serious views reflecting his own philosophy? Even his eloquent speech to the joint session of Congress after Kennedy's assassination urging passage of the civil rights bill as a tribute to President Kennedy did not entirely convince civil rights leaders and liberals in and out of Congress.

Perhaps these doubts and questions were to some degree a reflection of the enormous difficulties of getting effective legislation through the Congress. After all, President Kennedy had not pushed for such legislation in his first two years of office; he had viewed its enactment as a virtual impossibility. When he did so in 1963, pressed by events in the South and the urging of his brother, he did so reluctantly and with skepticism—not from lack of conviction in the rightness of the cause but from lack of confidence that it could succeed. Failure would have had a price.

Those of us in the Justice Department feared that LBJ, because of his vast legislative experience and knowledge of Congress, would not push hard in what could easily be regarded as a futile exercise. We felt, perhaps naively and contrary to historical precedent, that we could be successful. We had come to the conclusion, however, that even in the House success was not possible without Republican support, and RFK and Burke Marshall had wooed Congressman William McCulloch, the senior Republican on the Judiciary Committee, to support a "reasonable" bill.

The promise he exacted from us was that it not only be "reasonable" but that the administration give away nothing of importance in the Senate without his concurrence, and that we give Republicans credit for its passage. That promise was a rejection of past tactics that liberals in the House and civil rights leaders had questioned and, indeed, worked against. The common wisdom was to enact a strong bill in the House, then compromise in the Senate to avoid a filibuster—the technique Johnson had used in 1957 and 1960.

Given those facts, aggravated by his prickly relationship with RFK, President Johnson took the only politically realistic course. He told Bobby that the Justice Department had responsibility for the legislation and that he would do whatever Bobby asked him to do in support. While Bobby welcomed that charge, there was clearly ambiguity in it. Was LBJ pushing it on the Department to avoid responsibility for its failure? Or was it a genuine conviction that one could not change horses in midstream and that identifying the bill with JFK, as he generously did, and letting Robert Kennedy shepherd it through the House were the best political courses of action?

What is important in retrospect is that LBJ kept his word. It must have been extraordinarily difficult for such a political animal and skilled legislator to take guidance from the comparatively inexperienced people in the department, particularly Bobby. But it was extremely important in the House that he did. Just as LBJ had a certain distrust of the Republican leadership's keeping its commitments, so did that leadership have reciprocal feelings. In my view, the relatively hands-off policy (LBJ did help and gave advice freely, usually through Larry O'Brien) was essential to its passage in the House. LBJ was both prompt and generous in his praise of Republicans and Democrats alike.

At a reception in the White House shortly after passage of the bill in the House, LBJ pulled me aside and began to interrogate me about our plans for the bill in the Senate. I told him we planned to give away nothing and hoped to defeat a southern filibuster through cloture; together we went over, name by name, the possible votes. While he was—understandably—skeptical, he saw a possibility, albeit remote, of adding to the sixty-three votes we agreed were likely to get the necessary sixty-seven. From that moment on, despite his skepticism, he firmly took the position that we would get cloture. Coming from him, that position gained instant credibility.

In the Senate LBJ's actions were indispensable for passage and for defeating a filibuster. He understood instantly that the key to cloture and passage of a strong bill lay with the minority leader, Senator Everett Dirksen. Dirksen wanted around-the-clock debate to break the inevitable filibuster, but his successor as majority leader, Senator Mike Mansfield, declined, out of concern for the health of some of the older members. Most importantly, LBJ urged, persuaded, and cajoled the floor leader, Hubert Humphrey, to appreciate the importance of Dirksen and to praise him, with or without justification, as a great statesman and congressional leader, a man of vision and wisdom who acted in the public interest. President Johnson's ability to persuade Humphrey to act in this way was a key to success, and something perhaps only he could have done so effectively.

Humphrey organized the supporters brilliantly. The president used his good relationship with Dirksen to secure his support for a strong bill and cloture. He, and the White House staff, refused to negotiate specific terms and provisions of the bill; that was left to Justice. Dirksen, of course, was essential to success, but he faced a difficult job in getting the votes from the more conservative members of the Republican party. Based on past experience he expected Johnson to act pragmatically, to give up some provisions to help passage without cloture. The president adamantly refused, and Dirksen had to face the hard reality of choosing between the bill or a position that the public would label racist.

Most importantly, the president thus put his own reputation and his presidency on the line, by always taking firm positions and by assuring civil rights leaders and senators alike that his administration was committed to strong legislation, that no deals would be made, that the bill would not be weakened but would pass substantially as it had passed the House. As a result, leaders like Martin King, Roy Wilkins, John Lewis, Whitney Young, and others came to have confidence that LBJ meant what he said. Even liberals like Joe Rauh became convinced; with LBJ's leadership, confidence that victory was possible led to ever-increasing momentum for the bill.

But beyond this, it became more and more obvious that President Johnson not merely supported this legislation; he was committed to racial equality as a moral, not just a political, issue.

It is perhaps difficult today to appreciate the huge significance of the passage of the Civil Rights Act of 1964 and the seventy-one votes for cloture that made it possible. Many people deserve credit for this national turning point—this commitment by the nation to treat, at long last, its black citizens with dignity. But no one deserves more credit than the southern president who stood firm for what he had come to believe was not only right but essential for our democracy. LBJ had stayed in the background and let others—especially Humphrey and Dirksen—take the credit, but it was his steadfast support that made the Civil Rights Act possible. Civil rights, the War on Poverty, and education became collectively the bedrock of his domestic program. While LBJ often spoke of his dedication to the principles of the New Deal, he went far beyond them, not only in the struggle for racial equality in a formal sense—a huge achievement in itself—but in the programs that sought to give formulations reality.

With the passage of the 1964 act and the resignation of RFK to run for the Senate from New York, Burke Marshall and I began to consider how best to organize governmental efforts to promote equal rights. We felt that it was now important to promote programs that were the responsibility of other departments—Agriculture, HEW (Health, Education, and Welfare), HUD (Housing and Urban Development)—if blacks were to be given the opportunities for equality now open, we hoped, to all. To us it appeared that the role of the Department of Justice—limited to law enforcement and ensuring, through the courts, constitutional rights—would play at most a supporting role with respect to other departments. Most importantly, what Justice had been able to do when the attorney general's brother had been president and what it could now do in terms of influencing other departments to act was vastly different.

Our answer was to put coordination of all such programs in the White House, under Vice President Humphrey. He had the confidence of the civil rights leaders and the president, and we thought an executive order giving him this responsibility made sense. If nothing else, it gave the vice president an important governmental function that, in our view, would leave the president free to avoid the details. President Johnson did not like the idea at all and initially refused to sign the order we had drafted. His argument was mainly that the civil rights leaders had confidence in the department and would view this as a retreat from the administration's commitment to equal rights. Eventually he did sign the order, but reluctantly, and it never worked out. In retrospect I think his reluctance was borne of his own desire to play the leadership role and to get the recognition he richly deserved. But what defeated its merits was in part the urgency of events of December 1964 and January 1965.

Passage of the Civil Rights Act of 1964 did not, of course, put an end to the demands of civil rights leaders. It merely changed the focus from sit-ins in restaurants and department stores to voting. There were some quite strong provisions in the 1964 act on voting—provisions that in time might well have proven effective. But African Americans understandably were out of patience with delays and the often excessive time that it took to prevail in court. They wanted stronger medicine, and the cloture vote convinced them that it was time to seek it. As southern voting registrars continued to abuse literacy tests as a device to exclude black voters, pressure in the form of demonstrations and marches grew. President Johnson had numerous meetings with black leaders.

The Department of Justice and, I am sure, those working in the White House with Congress wanted relief from the stress and strain of civil rights legislation, which had taken well over a year to enact into law. I am sure the president, like his predecessor, had other legislation in his Great Society program that he had no desire to postpone. But civil rights leaders kept pressing, demonstrations kept increasing, and President Johnson, always the politician, thought a really strong voting rights bill was essential to both political and social progress in the South. He asked Justice to draft the strongest bill possible, although I think he was uncertain as to when he wished to send it to Congress. But I am certain that he wanted a civil rights bill that bore his name and reflected his leadership— one that once and for all would show the world where he stood on racial equality.

During the summer of 1964 almost a thousand college students from the North had gone to the South, especially Mississippi, to attempt to persuade black citizens to register to vote. They saw first-hand the reluctance of blacks to expose themselves to the wrath of whites by attempting to register. They saw the difficulties of efforts by the Justice Department to break the discriminatory use of literacy tests on a case-by-case basis in the courts. Thus the efforts of civil rights leaders, especially Robert Moses, and young idealists from the North exposed not only the problems of registering blacks to vote but, perhaps as importantly, the inability of the federal government to protect their efforts from the occasional violence reaction of Ku Klux Klan–related groups.

While the relative lack of violence that accompanied the 1964 act put the lie to the dire predictions of southern leaders about public accommodations, the pressure to secure the ballot free of white interference and threats grew stronger and more dangerous. It came to a head in Selma, Alabama, in early 1965. Selma had long been a target of the department because of its voter discrimination, and cases had been won, but results continued to be delayed and registration frustrated. Dr. King, in January, decided to make this small town on the Alabama River the focal point of demonstrations focused on voter registration. In King's words, blacks were "demanding the ballot" and were willing to go to jail by the thousands if necessary. In Dallas County's sheriff, James Clark, King had an ideal racist foil. In January and February the sheriff arrested blacks by the hundreds, including Dr. King and Ralph Abernathy, as they marched to the courthouse seeking to register blacks. The demonstrations spread to other towns, and the violent reaction of law enforcement officials, all recorded on national television, made voting rights in the South an urgent national issue. It culminated when Dr. King announced a fifty-mile march to Montgomery from Selma, though Governor George Wallace ordered it prohibited. On Sunday, March 7, some 600 blacks and a few whites sought to begin the march to Montgomery by crossing the Pettus Bridge over the Alabama River, only to be met by armed state troopers and Sheriff Clark's deputies. The bloody attack on the peaceful marchers was viewed on national television by millions.

One result of the unwarranted attack on King and his followers was demonstrations around the country by people understandably offended by what they had seen on TV. There were sit-ins in the White House and in the Department of Justice. Six hundred demonstrators paraded outside the White House demanding that the federal government do something to prevent bloodshed. The president, as committed to voting rights and peaceful demonstrations as the demonstrators themselves, wanted to protect the demonstrators in Alabama from the likes of Sheriff Clark and kept pressing me to say he had the constitutional power to send in troops. However, I did not believe we had enough evidence yet of the governor's unwillingness or inability to preserve law and order, as was necessary to justify federal intervention. Further, I thought it important that southern law enforcement officials, and governors, not be permitted to pass off the basic function of government—maintaining the peace in a constitutionally correct way—to the federal government.

The president agreed with this position, but it is difficult to support principles of federalism when citizens are being physically abused and beaten.

I was anxious to support the president in his commitment to civil rights and was aware of how deeply he was hurt by the demonstrations accusing him of lack of commitment because of his failure to send federal troops to protect Dr. King and his followers. In an effort to ease that burden, I held a press conference where I made it clear that it was I who said the constitutional authority to send troops to Alabama did not exist on the present facts and that I had repeatedly so advised the president. Obviously that position did not satisfy the demonstrators; abstract constitutional principles are never an answer to the immediate threats and fear of violence. But I think it did help the president for me to take some of the burden off his shoulders, and he was especially warm in his comments to me about the press conference.

The conference may also have had an unintended and unanticipated result. The next day—Friday, March 11—Governor Wallace asked LBJ for a meeting, presumably to discuss the demonstrations and the president's refusal to send federal troops to protect the march from Selma to Montgomery. The president immediately granted the request and met with the governor the next morning. Also, LBJ told me that he intended to send the voting rights bill to the Congress on Monday and that I should attend the meeting with Wallace and be prepared to give the press background on the bill.

Burke Marshall and I attended the meeting. Immediately before the meeting LBJ asked me to write down six demands he could make of Wallace. When I asked him what kind of demands, he replied: "I don't care. Make them as outrageous as you want." I did. I gave the president such demands as: desegregate today all the public schools in Alabama; abolish literacy tests; use the highway patrol to protect Dr. King on his march; and make sure all the blacks in Alabama are registered to vote. The president read them, nodded and smiled, and put the paper in his pocket. He then went to meet the governor as he entered the White House and escorted him to the Oval Office.

For almost an hour I had the privilege of seeing a master politician at work, and it was an unforgettable experience. The tall president, sitting in his rocking chair, towered over the slight governor, totally dominating him. To my amazement—and to Wallace's utter shock—LBJ actually used the demands I had provided him. The conversation went in part something like this:

> **LBJ:** George, did you see all those demonstrators outside the White House?
>
> **GW:** Oh, yes, Mr. President.
>
> **LBJ:** Wouldn't it be great if we could put an end to those demonstrations?
>
> **GW:** Oh, yes, Mr. President, that surely would.
>
> **LBJ:** Well, George, we could. Did you see all those reporters and TV cameras outside as you came in?
>
> **GW:** Yes sir, I did.
>
> **LBJ:** Well, George, why don't you and I go out and tell all those reporters that you've decided to desegregate all the schools in Alabama?
>
> **GW:** (Taken totally aback and almost stammering): But Mr. President, I can't do that. I don't control the schools in Alabama.
>
> **LBJ:** Don't shit me, George. I know who runs Alabama. [A pause] George, how do you think I'm doing in Vietnam?

And so forth—using in similar fashion most of the points I had written down. George Wallace, an experienced and capable politician, must have realized he had more than met his match, that he had been had. Most significantly, in my opinion, he had to be convinced that LBJ absolutely meant what he said about his dedication to equal rights for all. Wallace left by the back door. The president and I went to brief the press on the voting rights bill, which would be sent to the Congress on Monday. While LBJ may have hoped that Wallace would ask him to send troops to Alabama, and Wallace may have hoped that the president would join him in criticizing the demonstrators, I think the most significant aspect of the Wallace meeting lay in the fact that Johnson had decided before the meeting, and irrespective of its outcome, to send the strongest voting rights bill we could draft to Congress. Shrewdly he took advantage of public disgust at the actions of Sheriff Clark and the Alabama highway patrol and at the governor's failure to protect peaceful demonstrations by blacks. He focused public attention on Congress and the right to vote, thus diverting attention from his own refusal to send federal troops to Alabama.

The president in the same vein, had already decided to present the bill to Congress personally, in an address to a joint session. He called in the leadership on Sunday, and over the opposition of Mansfield and Dirksen, they issued him the invitation. On Monday evening he delivered one of his great political speeches, feverishly drafted up to the last possible minute by Richard Goodwin, putting all his presidential power and prestige behind a single bill.

It was in that speech that he linked himself publicly and irrevocably with the civil rights movement. At its most dramatic moment he raised both arms and declaimed: "And we shall overcome!" A moment of silence and then a huge spontaneous ovation rocked the House as the president of the United States invoked the words of the hymn of a thousand black demonstrations. That was the moment that LBJ became the leader of the civil rights movement—when the public, and especially its black citizens, realized that this tall southerner had made racial equality the touchstone of his presidency.

Johnson, always the expert politician, kept the pressure on. He told me to ask Emanuel Celler, the chairman of the House Judiciary Committee, to hold evening hearings, to emphasize the urgency of the legislation. I did so, and on Tuesday evening I was testifying before the whole committee explaining why we must act directly, with federal voting registrars if necessary, rather than rely on the courts, with their inevitable delays, to ensure the right to vote. At that moment LBJ had a lucky break, and in an amusing way, I was a part of it.

As I was testifying, the committee clerk suddenly announced, for all in a crowded committee room to hear, that the president wanted me on the phone. LBJ told me that Governor Wallace was on television saying he had asked the president for troops, since Alabama could no longer afford to protect its citizens; he wanted my advice. The cautious lawyer in me told me to tell him to do nothing until he received the governor's telegram and we could see exactly what it said. I returned to my testimony.

Perhaps ten minutes passed before the clerk again announced that the president wanted me on the telephone. This time President Johnson read me the telegram, and I told him that I thought it sufficient for him now to call the Alabama National Guard into federal service to protect the demonstrators. He asked me to dictate a response he could send to Wallace, and I did. Unfortunately the young woman he put on the phone did not take shorthand, and a few minutes later I was summoned to the phone once more to repeat my dictation. The result, of course, was the peaceful march by Dr. King and some 3,000 followers from

Selma to Montgomery, protected by the Alabama Guard in federal service.

Thus President Johnson prevailed on every front. He skillfully used the events of Selma to give momentum to a very strong voting rights bill, to identify himself strongly and unequivocally with civil rights for all Americans, and to manipulate George Wallace into inviting federal troops into Alabama. Politically, the latter was important. There would have been a huge southern resentment if the president had "invaded" the South. It took courage and skill to resist the pressure of civil rights leaders and demonstrators—especially when he sympathized with their demands—to send in troops before he had the clear constitutional right to do so.

After passage of the 1964 act, with its successful invocation of cloture, there was never serious doubt about the passage of the Voting Rights Act. Not only were southern members of Congress, especially in the Senate, demoralized, but no one—not even the most segregationist member—was willing to say publicly that it was proper to deny the vote to blacks. The debate centered around the propriety of poll taxes and literacy tests—the devices (unfairly applied and coupled with threats) used to prevent black voter registration. But, unlike the 1964 act, the administration had no promise of Republican support. That support depended on public opinion, and here the election results, with increased Democratic majorities in both Houses and the brilliance of LBJ's tying the bill to Selma, paid off.

Gerald Ford had replaced Charles Halleck as minority leader in the House, largely because of Halleck's support for the 1964 act, which, in the Committee of the Whole (where votes are not recorded), Ford had repeatedly—and unsuccessfully—led efforts to weaken that act. Now, Ford tried to gain Republican support for a somewhat weaker voting rights bill. The tactic failed when a number of Republicans defected on the ground that it appeared to put them on the side of Governor Wallace and Sheriff Clark at Selma. Similar tactics were employed by Senator Dirksen in efforts to modify the stronger—and they were very strong—provisions of the bill.

As in 1964, LBJ stood firm—which made our seemingly endless negotiations with Senator Dirksen and his staff relatively easy. Our tactic was to change the words without changing the substance, an approach that seemed to satisfy Dirksen's ego. Only on the elimination of the provision repealing poll taxes—a provision of questionable constitutionality if the

Supreme Court were to find poll taxes themselves constitutional—did Dirksen prevail on substance, and only then because Senator Mansfield and Justice shared his constitutional concerns. Civil rights leaders and liberals led by Senators Edward Kennedy and Philip Hart sought unsuccessfully to reinstate the poll tax prohibition. LBJ, opposed as he was to a poll tax, reluctantly—but wisely—sided with Mansfield, leaving the matter to the Supreme Court. Soon thereafter the Supreme Court found the tax itself unconstitutional, making the point moot and showing the correctness of the administration's view.

Southern senators continued—although halfheartedly, in view of the foreordained result—to offer weakening amendments until Senator Mansfield finally decided to call a halt to the feckless filibuster, and the Senate voted seventy to thirty to end debate. The House accepted the Senate version, and the voting rights bill became law some four months after its introduction by President Johnson.

Again the president seized the occasion to make a strong and emotional speech on civil rights. Electing to sign the bill in the Rotunda of the Capitol, he spoke of the long struggle for equality, ending by declaring that while "this is a victory for the freedom of the American Negro it is also a victory for the freedom of the American nation."

The South accepted the Voting Rights Act with only occasional and sporadic violence—tragic as that was—and began to register voters without massive use of federal registrars. The president had promised that if the law were complied with, federal registrars would be either not used or withdrawn, and the department did its utmost to make this statement come true. As always, the president wanted compliance with the law, not a huge enforcement problem. Also, he correctly foresaw that the vote in the hands of blacks would change southern politics irrevocably.

With the Voting Rights Act the southern caste system and legally sanctioned racial discrimination was put to an end. But, as the president clearly understood throughout, enforcement of formally equal political rights was the easy part of the racial problem to solve. The difficult part was to give blacks their share of economic progress and prosperity. Unfortunately, there was, and is, no easy answer that does not take time— more time than anyone wants. In June, LBJ had made his great speech at Howard University on how Negroes were "trapped . . . in inherent, gateless poverty," suffering "the consequences of ancient brutality, past injustice, and present prejudice." The president understood the problem well, but it was not soluble in the short term.

Ironically, the violence that followed the Voting Rights Act took place in the North and West—in Watts, and later in the District of Columbia, Chicago, Newark, and elsewhere. Civil rights leaders like Dr. King moved into northern ghettos, where they were challenged in their nonviolence by more militant leaders, such as Malcolm X, Elijah Muhammad, and other northern blacks who understood better than King the frustration and anger of young blacks in the slums of northern cities. Violence and riots did not deter LBJ or weaken his determination to create a Great Society in which blacks could share equality. His legislative program aimed at poverty and education, his appointment of commissions to study the problems of urban blacks, and his appointment of blacks to high governmental positions and Thurgood Marshall to the Supreme Court all evidenced his determination to continue the struggle—despite unrest and riots, Vietnam demonstrations, and the cooling of the enthusiasm of many northern whites when the racial problems moved north.

Many of the difficulties that LBJ tried to solve in his Great Society programs remain with us today. There is still a strong residue of racial prejudice—no longer overt but still there, nonetheless. We have a long distance yet to go. But there can be no question that it was Lyndon Johnson whose presidency showed the way, with courage, determination, and unparalleled legislative success.

If President Johnson were alive today, he would be proud of what has been accomplished but unhappy that more has not been done. I suspect his biggest disappointment would lie in the facts that educational opportunity is still far from equal and that with all our technological progress, we are not training the educated workforce this country needs. LBJ saw educational opportunity as basic to the other opportunities in life. He would see the tremendous success of programs like Head Start and wonder why we have not done much more to build on that success. He would be unhappy—but, I think, not surprised—that racial prejudice still exists; that politicians could exploit that prejudice covertly was obvious from the success in 1968 of George Wallace, who, unhappily, showed the way for others to emulate.

Another great success in most aspects was affirmative action. President Johnson would be unhappy at some of the mindless criticisms made today of programs designed to overcome unconscious racial prejudice and give qualified blacks a genuine chance in employment and higher education. He had two concerns: first, that through education blacks be made qualified for jobs on the same basis as whites; second, that qualified blacks be given equal opportunities. That is what affirmative action was all about, and he would have been pleased that many large corporations have such programs and that many universities have made it possible for qualified blacks to get the country's best education. He would, I believe, have been unhappy at the criticisms that have been made in California and at the decisions in the courts that have forbidden use of race as a factor in university admissions. He would have been opposed, of course, to quotas, for the simple reason that quotas are unrelated to qualifications.

If President Johnson were alive today, he would take satisfaction in seeing the progress that, in large measure thanks to him, this country has made. And as I have said, I think he would wish governmental programs to focus on education, health, and providing an escape from the mindless trap of poverty that so many blacks—and whites—are still in.

# The Wind at His Back: LBJ, Zephyr Wright, and Civil Rights
## *Lee White*

It is now more than thirty years since the close of the Lyndon Johnson administration, and historians' report cards have begun to come together to form an early consensus on that administration. In general, they give it a D-minus on Vietnam, an A in civil rights and education, and for the Great Society programs some high grades and some not-so-high grades.

With regard to civil rights, I had the great good fortune to have been assigned to that area by President Kennedy and to have remained on with President Johnson through March 1966. When JFK moved into the White House, civil rights leaders and African Americans in general sensed that there was a new attitude in the federal government and that doors would more readily swing open for consideration of their great concerns, and for them. Of course, they were correct.

The unanimous decision of the Supreme Court in *Brown v. Board of Education* in 1954, followed by the blockbusting Civil Rights Act of 1957 (blockbusting not because of its relatively gentle content but because it was passed at all) and by President Eisenhower's dispatch of troops to integrate Little Rock's Central High School, had all denoted progress and a greater willingness of the national government to address racial strife. But progress was painfully slow. John Kennedy, as candidate, courted black voters. His telephone call to the Rev. Martin Luther King, Jr., in jail in

Atlanta and his chiding of President Eisenhower for his failure to end discrimination in housing "with a stroke of the pen" were instrumental in a big turnout of black voters on election day. The black community could claim that but for its support, the election would have gone the other way. President Kennedy's reply was: "Yes, I know—every group tells me that, and they're all correct."

One of JFK's first actions was to establish the Committee on Equal Employment Opportunity and designate the vice president as its chairman. With his usual vigor and industriousness, LBJ talked Hobart Taylor, a brilliant lawyer and the son of one of his black friends and supporters in Texas, to be the staff director. With his committee of whites and blacks, lawyers and businessmen, and with Taylor's pushing spirit, the committee produced a program known as "Plans for Progress," which were in effect pledges by individual national corporations to increase their minority employees by agreed percentages over specified periods of time. The program was not without its critics, who contended that it was window dressing because there were no sanctions and that it was the equivalent of the federal government awarding "Good Housekeeping Seals of Approval." Word reached Bobby Kennedy, the attorney general, who passed on the criticism to JFK. I wound up with the assignment to check it out. Working with Taylor and George Reedy, an assistant of LBJ and later his press secretary, I went over the numbers and the nature of the Plans for Progress and concluded that basically the program was a step in the right direction, that there were no sweetheart deals, and that the participants on both sides were sincere. The major deficiency was that there was no statutory underpinning for the program and that it was not possible to require or enforce sanctions. Ultimately, Congress created the Equal Employment Opportunity Commission, with Franklin Delano Roosevelt, Jr., as its first chairman.

The next major activity involving the vice president was the series of leadership meetings President Kennedy held with various groups during the summer of 1963. Among the groups that met in the East Room of the White House were labor leaders, educators, religious leaders, lawyers, and business leaders (the only group that did not rise when the president entered the room). As the staff man handling the meetings, I was told by JFK to be sure that Bobby Kennedy, Assistant Attorney General for Civil Rights Burke Marshall, and the vice president attended. With respect to LBJ, President Kennedy said, "I want everyone to know that the entire federal establishment is concerned that we do more, and besides he's from Texas and that means more than hearing from a son of Massachusetts." I'm not quite certain, but he might also have added, "If this whole effort goes down the drain, I want him in on it."

I worked with agency and department heads to develop the lists of invitees and prepared a one-or-two-page memo for the president explaining who was to be there and the points that he might touch on. This was before the days of Xerox copies, and on occasion I would neglect to bring a carbon copy for LBJ (not out of orneriness or disdain, but plain forgetfulness—when your boss is the president, the vice president is not always at the top of your agenda). In any event, a few minutes before the meeting was to begin, the president would be going over the memo (sometimes he used most of the points, sometimes practically none); I would be standing in front of his desk, behind me the six-foot, four-inch LBJ looking over my shoulder (I am five feet, seven inches) saying, "Do ya think I could get one of those copies some time?" (When LBJ became president, he seemed to have forgotten every lapse or slight on my part.) The meetings played a significant role in building support for subsequent legislative initiatives.

Inspired by Louis Martin, one of the shrewdest political operatives to be involved in presidential politics, and a black man, the Kennedy administration had sent to Congress in the spring of 1963 legislation to eliminate discrimination in public accommodations. The legislation had really not gone very far. After the assassination of JFK, the new president made this legislation a top priority. LBJ, who had a flair for symbolism, would tell every group, large or small, about the unbelievable fact that when the Johnson family's cook, Zephyr Wright, and her husband had driven the Johnson sedan from Washington to Texas and back during congressional recesses, they could not go into any restaurants or use restrooms in gas stations. It was a dramatic and effective way of bringing discrimination down to reality—a great principle was at stake, but not being able to use the toilet was a powerful argument for eliminating discrimination in public accommodations.

While on the subject of symbolism, within days of taking over as president, LBJ said to me that he was thinking about inviting the group of major civil rights leaders to spend a day at his ranch in Texas; what did I think about it? I said he'd never invited them to dinner while he was vice president, and that it would have a phony, staged look to it. He didn't invite them. I now believe that the symbolic benefits would have outweighed questions about his motives for such an occasion. Another early issue was what to do about the fact that his daughter Lynda lived in a segregated dormitory at the University of Texas in Austin. I said that since she was planning to come to live in the White House at the end of the semester, why attract attention to what no one had noted or complained about? Why leave himself open to the charge that it was all right while he was vice president but not when he became president?

LBJ's mastery in achieving legislative goals was an acknowledged fact of political life during his career. There were a number of facets to his prodigious skill. While majority leader in the Senate, he knew every member's political situation at home, what issues and projects were near and dear to his or her heart, what committee assignment he or she coveted, and what time of day was best to negotiate with him or her. He knew the gritty details of key legislation; he knew the sense of accomplishment that the body would have collectively in a record of achievement; and he knew how to count. But in my view, central to his technique was single-mindedness. He would establish a target and focus every action and thought on that objective until it was accomplished; then another issue would be elevated to the target position. This was his approach to the civil rights bill of 1964, but the clearest illustration was the education bill in 1965.

The civil rights leadership group had asked for a meeting with LBJ to discuss something that they were unhappy about. I don't recall the problem, but as soon as the group had assembled in his office and had been properly greeted, the president said to me, "Tell Larry O'Brien [his congressional liaison] to come down with his tally sheet." He then turned to the group and said, "I understand you have some bone to pick with me, and I'm sure it's something that can be worked out, but it can't be as important as a vote we're having tomorrow on an education bill. Now, you know that there's nothing more important to your people than that education bill. Now, Larry O'Brien's going to read off the names of the House members that we need to pass the bill, and I want you to tell him which of you can get each of the doubtful votes to impress on them the importance of the bill so that we can get this thing passed." With that, O'Brien started down his alphabetical state list. LBJ would say, "Now, which of you are going to take that guy?" They each took lobbying assignments and left to do them. The bill passed; I'm sure there was another meeting to discuss the original problem.

The leadership group consisted of Phillip Randolph, the distinguished and stately former head of the Pullman porters union (frequently his assistant, Bayard Rustin, would attend in his absence); Roy Wilkins, head of the NAACP; Dr. Martin Luther King, Jr., head of the Southern Christian Leadership Conference (occasionally the Reverend Ralph Abernathy would substitute for Dr. King); Whitney Young, head of the Urban League; James Farmer, head of the Congress of Racial Equality; Dorothy Height, head of the National Association of Negro Women; and John Lewis, of the Student Non-Violent Coordinating Committee (now a congressman from Georgia). This was a most impressive group of individuals, and as one might guess, sometimes a bit of elbowing went on among its members. Dr. King, following his dramatic and powerful speech in August 1963 at the Lincoln Memorial, and after receiving the Nobel Peace Prize, became a little more difficult to deal with, in the sense that he would not speak to me directly, only through his assistant, Wyatt Walker. Relations obviously suffered when Dr. King began to oppose the Vietnam War.

In general, the leadership—even if there were some matters where they were not in agreement on details or timing—knew that there was a sympathetic and hugely successful LBJ working on behalf of the blacks in this country. However, that did not prevent an explosive situation from developing at the 1964 Democratic Convention in Atlantic City, New Jersey. The regular delegation from Mississippi had been put together by the state's white political leadership, headed by Senator James Eastland. But a rump group, led by Aaron Henry and Fannie May Hamer, claiming that the "regular" delegation had not been legally selected, showed up in Atlantic City. President Johnson was obviously unhappy with the confrontation. As I recall, a compromise was hammered out under which clear procedures would be established for the future.

This confrontation was symptomatic of the basic problem LBJ faced. As Senate majority leader, he worked with and was supported by the southerners in the Senate, especially the senior members, who were solidly entrenched committee chairmen. Senator Richard Russell of Georgia had been a mentor to LBJ when he first came to the Senate and had been instrumental in LBJ's rising to the majority leader position. There was no way that they would or could go along with civil rights legislation. But the nation was ready for movement, and LBJ, adroitly using the death of President Kennedy and every wily legislative device he could put his hands on, was able to pull it off. He was aided in the Senate by the crucial assistance he got from the Republican minority leader, Senator Everett Dirksen of Illinois. Dirksen was a cagey character, and we all speculated about what LBJ had promised him in return for his support. To be fair about it, Dirksen would not have supported the legislation just to gain leverage or commitments on presidential appointments. But why not take advantage of a golden opportunity? Two slick characters like LBJ and Dirksen negotiating would have been a sight to behold.

It is no secret that Lyndon Johnson was a very complex human being. He could be charming, outrageous, extremely thoughtful and considerate, vindictive, sensitive, profane, sentimental, mean, demanding, overbearing, persuasive, crafty, and shrewd; above all, he was intelligent. He wanted to move as rapidly as possible to achieve his goals. His political instincts and experiences told him that political capital could not be put in a bank and drawn out as needed—rather, it was an evanescent commodity that had to be used while one possessed it. One cannot be sure, but his family medical history, coupled with the massive heart attack he suffered while majority leader in the Senate, must have contributed to his desire to move as far and as fast as possible. (He would almost always take a nap in the afternoon for forty-five minutes or an hour, waking up refreshed and ready to go for another five or six hours. I believe he wondered why his staff seemed a bit bushed toward the end of the day.)

High on his agenda were the issues of racial discrimination and problems of the poor. His empathy for the blacks, who had been treated so badly, and for the poor, regardless of their color, was deep in him. He was willing to do what had to be done to solve these fundamental problems. However, the next civil rights target was to secure the vote for the black community.

LBJ believed firmly that if blacks were able to vote, political officeholders and office seekers would pay attention to them. Moving with speed and trying to capitalize on the passage of the 1964 Civil Rights Act, he began the push for voting rights legislation that would wipe out the voting barriers that faced black citizens in most southern states. Although blacks had the legal right to vote, for the most part the impediments in the southern states to voting made a mockery out of the legal right. The poll tax had been eliminated, but literacy and other barriers were in place. It is axiomatic that where the ballot box is used effectively, change can be achieved. LBJ knew this was the way to go. He also knew that the price would be to lose the South to the Republicans at least for a generation or two. That was not a cheerful prospect, but he knew in his gut that it had to be done. (He was, of course, correct, but after a generation, it appears that the southern states are beginning to become more competitive for Democratic candidates.)

As is frequently the case, events that are neither planned nor capable of being controlled can have profound effects. Thus the march on Selma, Alabama, which resulted in bloody scenes of violence on national television, offered President Johnson the opportunity to gain support for voting rights legislation, and he knew how to make the most of the opportunity. Speaking of television, I can offer a sidebar story to the legislative history. One Sunday afternoon while working in my yard, an idea popped into my head. The next morning I told Bill Moyers about it and suggested he pass it on to the president—he would consider it more favorably if it came from Moyers. Moyers said I should be the one. In any event, I did go to LBJ and suggest that instead of sending the "Message on Voting Rights to Congress" in written form, which was the standard method, he might address Congress, and incidentally the American public, in person before a joint session of Congress. There were practically no precedents other than the annual State of the Union messages (though President Franklin Roosevelt had addressed the Congress immediately after the bombing of Pearl Harbor); nevertheless, LBJ arranged for Speaker John McCormack to extend an invitation to him to address the Congress at nine o'clock in the evening.

President Johnson was no great orator, but that night he was at his best. He gave a potent speech, which ended dramatically with "And we shall overcome." The legislation has greatly changed the political landscape. But if the nation has come a long way in dealing with racial problems, there is yet perhaps a greater way to go. The metaphor of the half-full and half-empty glass comes to mind.

An example of how he operated took place the night of the voting rights speech. My reward for the suggestion to televise the speech rather than deliver it in writing was to pick up the civil rights leaders and escort them to a reserved gallery in the House chamber to listen to it. Back at the White House after the speech, there was a celebratory atmosphere; it was obvious that the speech had hit the bull's-eye. The place was jumping—there may even have been a few drinks passed around. In that joyous environment, at about eleven o'clock, the president said to Larry O'Brien, "Have you seen Manny Cellars [chairman of the House Judiciary Committee] to arrange for hearings?" He said to me, "Have you called Ben

Bradlee [managing editor of the *Washington Post*] to urge the *Post* to write a favorable editorial?" He knew about momentum. He also knew about the evanescence of political power. He wanted to get as much accomplished as he could while he had the wind at his back.

It is frequently difficult to know what an individual has done, but it is far trickier to attempt to discover that person's motives. More often than not, there is not a single motive but rather a number, some of which may be in conflict. Many factors moved President Johnson to make himself the boldest and most successful champion of civil rights since the Civil War—President Abraham Lincoln stands alone at the national summit. In candor, I must note that I never discussed the subject with LBJ. Those I offer are speculative, based on working with him, watching his agile mind strategize and develop tactics, and hearing what he said in formal speeches and in informal and relaxed conversations.

In the first instance, I believe his moral compass simply told him that discrimination was wrong. He had heard it from his parents. Although he took a Texas politician's position early in his career, he was after all, a Franklin Roosevelt Democrat. He secured passage of a civil rights bill in 1957 creating the Civil Rights Commission; here too there was a mixture of motives, but in this case his legislative wizardry produced the first legislation in nearly a hundred years. It was wrong that as fine and decent a woman as Zephyr Wright had to suffer such indignity and inconvenience because of the color of her skin.

I believe LBJ was anxious to demonstrate that he was a national president, not a southern or regional president. When he asked me to go to the Federal Power Commission in 1966, he made the point, saying the position was especially difficult for him to fill because he was perceived as a president from Texas, a gas-producing state. He wanted fair and proper, not skewed, administration of the Natural Gas Act. Earlier I noted that President Kennedy now wanted his vice president at meetings with various leadership groups to promote national support for civil rights and to show that a politician from Texas supported the effort.

Following the martyred, charismatic President Kennedy was not easy. But the legislation proposed by the Kennedy administration had really not made much progress. Thus Lyndon Johnson found an opportunity to demonstrate his legislative prowess by pushing it through—skillfully using, by the way, the assassination as reason to provide in the program a tribute to the slain president.

Finally, there was an election coming in the fall of 1964. President Johnson knew that his successful push for a civil rights bill would likely lose the southern states; progress on a legislative front could be helpful to carry the Northeast, the industrial states of the Middle West, and the far West. The landslide that actually occurred made the strategy, if indeed there was one, unnecessary, but it's fair to speculate that this factor was somewhere in the mix.

A proud and vain man, LBJ was humiliated, I am sure, by the reaction to the Vietnam War. In 1968, about the only places he could go to speak without facing jeering protesters were military facilities. When Minnesota Senator Eugene McCarthy ran a close race in the New Hampshire primary, President Johnson decided not to seek reelection and retired to Texas. Regardless of the inherited nature of that war and the optimistic, if inaccurate, advice of the military, he was the fall guy.

There was a strong feeling that the Johnson administration would be deemed by history to have been a failure because of Vietnam. That was indeed, the early perception. Today, after more than thirty years, the perceptions are changing. John Kenneth Galbraith, the ever-popular and articulate economist, a former ambassador to India in the Kennedy years, and a very early and outspoken critic of the Vietnam War, addressed a gathering at the LBJ Library in Austin. He regretted those who had allowed the war to become the defining event of that period (including himself) had done far too little to correct the record. In Galbraith's view, "Lyndon Johnson was the most effective advocate of humane social changes in the United States in [the twentieth] century." George McGovern, the senator from South Dakota and the Democratic candidate for president in 1972, was another sharp critic of the war. In a letter to the *New York Times*, he aligned himself with Professor Galbraith, writing "I now regret not devoting more time praising the Johnson record at home."

Were Lyndon Johnson given the opportunity to view the United States today, my guess is that he would be somewhat pleased but surely disappointed. The thoughts of McGovern and Galbraith would bring a smile to his face. He would be overjoyed that Head Start was still alive, but he would fret that it was underfunded. He would probably be appalled at the drug scenes and at efforts to abolish affirmative action, but encouraged by the integration of the armed services. He would be aghast at the continuing numbers of poverty, especially in this powerful country. His advice would be, "Let's get going, we've a lot of ground to cover."

# Retreat to the Ranch: Johnson in Retirement

When Johnson left the White House on January 20, 1969, he retreated to his beloved ranch on the Pedernales River. He died suddenly of a heart attack on January 22, 1973. Harry Middleton describes the president's years in retirement before his untimely death.

# The Lion in Winter: LBJ in Retirement
## *Harry Middleton*

Concern that he might not live to finish a second term was one of the factors president Johnson pondered as he made his decision not to seek reelection in 1968. A decade earlier he had suffered a massive heart attack, and his family had a history of males dying early. As it happened, he lived two days beyond when that term would have ended.

Those four years out of the public eye after forty years in the spotlight were marred by failing health but for the most part were filled with small pleasures and quiet satisfactions. Lady Bird called them the "milk and honey years." Reports of a frustrated and unhappy emperor who had lost his empire do not square with the memories of those who shared that time with him.

During his days in power, he had made the Texas hill country part of the national scene. Those who watched the driving force of a leader who sought to launch a social revolution with an avalanche of legislation and looked for the wellsprings of his passion, his concern, and his energy found them in the land where he had been born. During those years, he had proudly demonstrated his deep affection for that land and its resources. Presidents, chancellors, and prime ministers had dined in the ranch house where his forbearers had gathered for family festivities; had been treated to the sectional epicurean pleasures of cabrito and pinto beans; had been entertained by high school choirs and country dancers. The places of interest they were taken to see were the coliseums, the Place d'Étoiles and the Versailles, of the hill country—the German houses of Fredericksburg, the forts at Johnson City, and always the pastures, where deer leaped at dusk and where the land projected in the day's last glimmering light an endless promise of serenity. Cabinet officers and aides were summoned from their desks in Washington to chairs under a giant live oak on the Pedernales River to hammer out programs that would combat poverty, advance education, and certify the civil rights of the oppressed.

Now he presided over a ranch instead of a nation, but he gave much the same attention to laying irrigation pipe, installing fences, and even the production and sale of eggs that he had once invested in statecraft. He created a green oasis in the land of rocks and cactus. Before his time was up, he saw to it that the ranch upon which for a while history had turned would be given to the American people.

There were other activities as well to fill those four years. He went to football games and dances, and he proudly took second seat to his wife as she ceremoniously gave awards to road workers who had preserved the wild flowers that color the land beside Texas highways. He supervised the compilation of his memoirs—his account of the major events of his presidency. He watched with care and interest the birth of a school of public affairs that bore his name and would train young men and women for public service, and the construction of the library where he would deposit the papers and memorabilia of four decades of public life.

I was a witness to, and participant in, a couple of those activities. Along with several other former staff members, I helped him compile his memoirs. We did the writing, usually based on observations he made, and then rewrote based on his editing. Some of it was fun. His initial reflections as we discussed what should go into particular chapters were lively and colorful.

Planning the chapter on Medicare, he told me about the occasion when Wilbur Cohen telephoned him from the Capitol with the news that the House Ways and Means Committee planned to report out a bill even stronger than the White House had submitted. How would the president react to that? LBJ's reply, as he recounted it to me, was, "I'd run get my brother." One of his hill country stories was about a man applying for a job as railway switchman who was asked what action he would take if two trains were racing toward each other on the same track. The man replied that he would get his brother, "because my brother has never seen a train wreck." "I told Wilbur," LBJ told me, "that neither my brother or anyone else had ever seen a bill get strengthened in a House committee."

That story stayed in the book, although perhaps it should not have. When the chapter was in draft form, the president told me to send a copy to Wilbur Cohen for his comment. Wilbur called me after he had read it and had one major change to suggest: "That isn't when the president told me the train wreck story. It was on another occasion." I dutifully reported that to Johnson, who instructed me, "You go ask Wilbur whose book this is." Such episodes were rare. Bob Hardesty and I tried to preserve LBJ's initial reflections with a tape recorder, but when Johnson saw the machine running the prose changed. All the folksiness disappeared, and the words became more ponderous. Our efforts to re-create his comments from memory didn't work either; he considered them not sufficiently "presidential." I rode with him around the ranch one day trying desperately to take down each word of his musings about the young people who had marched and chanted against him outside the White House gates. It was an eloquent and moving dissertation on the tragedy of history in which he and they had been caught together. Those words did not make it into the book either—but today they hang on a wall in the LBJ Library as part of the exhibit on Vietnam.

Particularly on Vietnam, he wanted to get it all down, all the memoranda and notes, the options considered in endless discussions. With it all laid out, he believed—at least he hoped—that history would see the hellish dilemmas as he had.

At his request, I became director of the library in early 1970. For the first year the thrust was to get the building completed in time for a May 1971 dedication and opening. About a month before D day, Johnson suddenly became concerned that the exhibits contained no mention of the controversies that had swirled through his presidency. "That was a very contentious time," he told me, "and we have to be aware of that. I don't want another damn credibility gap." So an instant controversy display was created, detailing the vivid arguments of the sixties—over the passage of Medicare, federal aid to education, civil rights, and, high on the list, of course, Vietnam. It was completed with about a week to spare, and LBJ was generally satisfied with it—with one exception. "I got a lot of mean letters," he said. "Let's show the meanest letter I ever got."

Archivists started pouring through the mail that had flooded the White House, sifting out the unfriendly pieces. I would show them to Johnson, whose reaction invariably was, "I know I got meaner letters than that." After a couple of days he said, "Let me see those letters." The archivists brought up a box of the critical correspondence, and he rifled through all those rancorous reminders of a tumultuous time. Finally, with a flourish, he handed me a postcard from a man in California. It read: "I demand that you as a gutless son of a bitch resign as president of the United States." "You can't get much meaner than that," he said, and that card became the final piece to be inserted into the exhibit on the controversies of the sixties.

"Now what are we going to do?" The president asked me eight days after the library had opened its doors to the public. Throughout the year we had had conversations that had given me a pretty good idea of what he wanted the library to be—in addition to a museum for the public and a study center for scholars, a place where speakers and conferences would explore important issues. I had not given it much conscious thought, but an idea had been formed, apparently lying dormant until it was activated by LBJ's restless desire to be moving on. I suggested that we select the papers on education as the first group to open for research and at their opening assemble experts for a symposium on the future of education.

The words were barely out of my mouth when Johnson said, "Let's do that as soon as we can. How long will it take to open the papers?" I picked a figure out of the air—six months. "We'll open those papers and we'll have a conference on education in six months," he said. "Then we'll follow that right up with the same thing on civil rights."

Processing papers is an archival exercise not readily understood by the layman, which I very definitely was. It is a general rule that papers that tend to be unduly embarrassing or harmful to living persons are to be closed during that person's lifetime. Obviously, this is not an exact science, but when there is a question someone has to make the final decision. In a library, that individual is the director. So as the processing of the education papers went on, the questions needing a decision came to me. The ones I could not immediately answer piled up on my desk.

Through these months, LBJ had given considerable attention to the formation of the symposium but none to the papers. But shortly before the conference was to begin he abruptly asked about them. When he learned that some had to be kept closed, he wanted examples. He was not impressed with the stack of examples on my desk. He wanted everything open. He was concerned that we might be too cautious about his image: "Good men have been trying to protect my reputation for forty years, and not a damn one has succeeded. What makes you think you can?" Then, sensing that I might be a bit dubious, he said that if I ever thought I had evidence that he did not mean what he was saying, "here's what I want you to do. I want you to call me. I'll be waiting for your call. I want you to say, 'One of us is full of shit and let's decide right now who it is.'"

The education symposium took place in January 1972. LBJ loved it, sitting in the front row through every session. Delivering the concluding remarks, he gave voice to the Johnson presidential philosophy: "This country has the money to do anything it has the guts to do and the will to do."

He was always a step ahead. As we approached our first anniversary, I happily reported to him that we would end the year having had 750,000 visitors, more than the other libraries combined. His response was pure Johnson: "Why not a million?"

In connection with the civil rights symposium, we planned to have a small exhibit displaying the major civil rights bills that had been passed during the Johnson administration. When I told him about it, he said, "What about the Emancipation Proclamation? Let's get that. Nobody around here has ever seen it." We got it and put it on display in the library.

The civil rights symposium, in December 1972, would be Lyndon Johnson's last public appearance. He had had two heart flare-ups in those retirement years, one quite recently, and his doctors had advised him not to make the trip from the ranch for this conference. But he came. Many of the giants of the old civil rights movement were there too: Earl Warren (who gave the keynote address), Clarence Mitchell, Roy Wilkins, Roy Innis, and Hubert Humphrey. They had come through a good many political wars together: the majority leader and his liaison to the liberal wing of the Senate; the president and his vice president, who had together tasted the triumph of the Great Society and then suffered the divisions that Vietnam inflicted on personal relations and political alliances, as on the country at large. In August, on LBJ's birthday, Humphrey had written him: "I have given you some difficult moments. These have not been easy times for either of us, but Mr. President, I was very proud to serve you—to be your vice president. I am eternally grateful for the opportunity that was mine to share even ever so little in what was planned and completed." Johnson responded: "If historians do note that we made life better for the American people, they will give credit to a vice president—and before that a senator—who was a compassionate man of the people."

Now they were together again, allies once more in a cause to which both had given their best in better days. Some of the New Turks were there as well: Vernon Jordan, who LBJ thought was presidential material; Barbara Jordan, an obscure political figure outside Texas whom he championed and invited to White House conferences; and Julian Bond. Just a few years before, Bond had demonstrated in the streets against Johnson because of Vietnam. Now he took to the podium with a different message: "When the forces demanded and the mood permitted," he said to a hushed auditorium, "for once an activist, human-hearted man had his hand on the levers of power and a vision beyond the next election. He was there when we and the nation needed him, and oh, by God, do I wish he was there now."

When Johnson ascended the stage in the final minutes of the conference, his step was labored, his speech was slow. He slipped a nitroglycerin tablet into his mouth. But then the adrenaline began to flow, and for a while he was vintage LBJ again, telling stories out of his hill country memory, bringing together the two opposing factions represented in the audience, exhorting them all to unite for the next step, bringing them together with the rallying cry of the civil rights movement that had stirred the whole nation when he had sounded it before the Congress just a few years before: "We shall overcome."

In January he attended a memorial service for one of his friends, held in a massive cathedral. Funerals always depressed him, particularly those heavy with liturgy and incense. "When I die," he said to Lady Bird the night he returned, "I don't want just our friends who come in their private planes to be there. I want the families in their pickup trucks too." When he was buried at his ranch ten days later, they were all there, the men of influence who had shared his days of power, and his rancher neighbors. Before the burial, his body lay in state in the LBJ Library. For twenty-four hours long lines of people passed by his casket. Many in those lines were young people who such a short time before had marched against him in the streets.

Lady Bird stood by the casket to greet those who came through. One young man, bearded and frayed, bowed to her and said, out of whatever jumble of feeling and emotion, "I'm sorry." Lady Bird said to him, "It's all right. He wanted to change things, too."

I had members of the staff with clickers counting those who came that day and night. I was asked why, and I said, "Because I feel sure that some where, some time, he's going to ask me how many were there."

# Epilogue: Is the Beautiful Woman Really Dead? The Legacy of Lyndon Johnson and His Great Society

In 1971 Johnson remarked:

> I figured when my legislative programs passed Congress, that the Great Society had a real chance to grow into a beautiful woman. And I figured her growth and development would be as natural and inevitable as any small child's. In the first year, as we got the laws on the books, she'd begin to crawl. Then in the second year, as we got more laws on the books, she'd begin to walk, and the year after that, she'd be off and running, all the time growing bigger and healthier and fatter. And when she grew up, I figured she'd be so big and beautiful that the American people couldn't help but fall in love with her, and once they did, they'd want to keep her around forever, making her a permanent part of American life, more permanent even than the New Deal. But now . . . everything I've worked for is ruined. . . . It's a terrible thing to sit by and watch someone else starve my Great Society to death. She's getting thinner and thinner and uglier and uglier all the time; now her bones are beginning to stick out and her wrinkles are beginning to show. Soon she'll be so ugly the American people will refuse to look at her; they'll stick her in a closest to hide her away and there she'll die. And when she dies, I too, will die.[1]

We will conclude by asking a number of questions. Did the dream die with the dreamer in 1973 when Johnson prematurely passed away? That is, was the elder George Bush correct in 1991 when he called the Great Society dead? Has the "beautiful woman" really died, or can she, in the new millennium, be resurrected and reinvented so that the president's dream will live on? Maybe, as Richard Goodwin speculated in his *Remembering America* in reference to Johnson's vision, ". . . if we open Lyndon Johnson's closest we will not find a corpse, but a sleeping princess ready to be restored." "Of course," Goodwin argued, "she will need a new wardrobe. Styles have changed. But not beauty, not the ideal of beauty."[2] Perhaps Goodwin was right. Maybe ideals never die.

Ben Wattenberg and Joseph Califano complete the anthology with two perspectives on the legacy of the Great Society and the Johnson years. Both address the same questions: Where do we go from here? What business is left unfinished?

## Notes

1. Quoted in Doris Kearns Goodwin, *Lyndon Johnson and the American Dream* (New York: St. Martin's Press, 1991), 286–87.

2. Richard Goodwin, *Remembering America* (New York: Harper Perennial Library, 1989), 427.

# The Great Society's Bum Rap
## Ben Wattenberg

Some of my best friends are conservatives and neoconservatives. I find that most of them are quite nice people, intelligent and openminded.

It's true that most of them believe in radical ideas like offering poor children government funds to attend private schools if the public schools aren't functioning. Most believe in the partial privatization of Social Security, a major effect of which would be that those Americans in the lower 50 percent of the income distribution would get to own equities, just as most everyone reading this volume already does. They believe that deregulation of the economy, often opposed by the big businesses targeted for deregulation, helps set up robust competition that increases economic efficiency and lowers prices for consumers, as does increased free trade. They approved of welfare reform because they believed the old system was trapping poor people in a web of dependence. Similarly, they believe that in the long term, racial preferences and disguised quotas do not promote civil rights or benefit minorities but stir a still simmering pot. Many of them, probably most of them, are in favor of legal abortion, as am I, albeit with some greater restrictions, and notwithstanding the fact that they find the legalisms of the actual five-to-four case of *Roe v. Wade* troubling. And so it goes. You may agree or disagree with these sorts of positions. I agree with most—but these are not nut-case prescriptions, and in any event, modern conservatism is in many ways at odds with itself. The untold story of American politics is that while the country has moved to the right, the right has moved toward the center.

In fact, I confess that, when asked, I say I am a neoconservative. With that, I'm still a registered Democrat, although I must say that when Al Gore told a black church audience on the Sunday before election that Bush style strict constructionism in the Supreme Court would take us back toward the slavery-era Constitution, which counted blacks as three fifths of a person, I came pretty close to saying, "I've Had It." I stay a Democrat in some large measure because I don't see much conflict between my views and those of most registered Democrats in America today (I speak of voters, not pols or self-anointed leaders). Most important, for the purposes of this essay, I don't see much conflict between my current views and those espoused by President Johnson during the years I worked on the White House staff. I supported the "Great Society" then; I support most of it now. (No one's perfect, not even President Johnson.) The big problems of liberalism and the Democratic party, as I see it, came about post-LBJ.

But I am a marked man. Many of my friends, these conservatives and neoconservatives, think the Great Society was very bad news. I have come to believe that the problem is largely one of political vocabulary, not substance.

I moderated a panel discussion recently at a large meeting of foundations, mostly conservative. One of the panelists mentioned, matter of factly, that his institution's goal was "dismantling" the Great Society. Gently, as is my wont, I mentioned that he didn't know what he was talking about and that he wouldn't want to do it even if he could, which he couldn't.

At dinner, I sat next to the president of another conservative foundation, a man of intellect, honor, and vision. He referred to the statement I just mentioned and, in a more moderate way, and said that in principle he agreed with the panelist that the Great Society had been a bad turn toward overly centralized government, and the quicker we got on the right road the better off America would be.

What's bothering them?

Was it the Civil Rights laws of 1964, 1965, and 1968? No, no—in fact, the shrewder ones like to point out that the "Solid South" of that day was solidly prosegregation and solidly Democratic.

Was it Medicare? Was it Social Security? (LBJ raised the minimum payment from fifty dollars per month to a hundred per month, which, as I reckon it, was a 100 percent increase for the elderly poor.) No. Social Security became law two-thirds of a century ago, long before their time. Medicare became law a third of a century ago. Some older conservatives, although not neoconservatives, may have been against it then on principle. Now they are concerned it will "go broke," but then again, most "wonks" are concerned about that, regardless of their party or ideological label. And in any event, most assuredly the conservative elected leaders are not against these programs. Indeed, they swear upon stacks of Bibles to defend the basic programs for the elderly against all enemies; in fact, to "save" them is a top priority.

Was it the "War on Poverty?" Well, many conservatives think poverty won that war. But their elected officials continue to endorse many of the LBJ programs; Head Start is one prominent example. Was it environmental activism of the Great Society? No. Much of the original conservationist ethic comes out of the conservative playbook. Greater environmental regulation was needed, but many conservatives think that environmentalism as a cause movement became a runaway train, doing too much, too fast, in a wrongheaded expensive way, and couched it in extremist and apocalyptic language. Was it greater funding for medical research through the National Institutes of Health? Certainly not; these folks get sick as much as liberals do.

Was it the war in Vietnam? Of course, many conservatives have problems with the way LBJ fought the war. But compared to the liberals of my acquaintance, they are "LBJ All the Way." In fact, many of them were almost as anticommunist as President Johnson himself, and those who weren't, became so. Was it feminism? Most of the conservative women I know work in the paid labor force, although they're more likely to be in the private sector than liberal women.

So why do many of them scorn the Great Society so?

When you probe, this is about what you get: the Great Society yielded runaway liberalism; values eroded; America became "coarser"; poor people became more dependent; crime went up; punishment went down; illegitimacy soared; America turned isolationist; quotas, race, gender and ethnic preferences, and busing upset the social order; fiscal discipline eroded; government became more pervasive in our lives—merely to begin a very long list.

It's a bum rap. And it's not a bum rap because all that didn't happen. It happened, all right. Author Francis Fukuyama has described the era as "The Great Disruption." Richard Scammon and I wrote about it in our 1970 book *The Real Majority*. We called it "The Social Issue." But the question I ask is this: Did this Great Disruption flow from the Great Society?

I think not. There was sea change in the mindset of liberal Democrats. But that erupted and reached full flower post-Johnson. That change had some salutary effects. Some are mentioned above. But some of the changes engendered in that disruptive era were a long way from salutary and, I would submit, a long way from LBJ's Great Society.

There was no "soft on crime" legislation proposed by the Johnson administration. "Busing to achieve racial balance" was not yet an issue. Pornography was dealt with as a state or local issue. Most movie actresses wore full complements of clothes on screen. The War on Poverty was designed as an anti-welfare strategy, "a helping hand, not a handout." President Johnson did give one speech (at Howard University) that hinted at an affirmative-action program that might be construed as endorsing preferences, but it was a complex address, principally based on an "outreach" concept, not outright preferences.

LBJ was a committed internationalist, just like every other post–World War II president, of either party. To the best of my knowledge President Johnson did not do drugs, and the prominent people who did tended to hate President Johnson.

So where does all that anti–Great Society stuff come from? We might do well to consider some other players in the game, most of whom came to greater prominence and power in the immediate aftermath of the LBJ presidency. Consider these, briefly: the Supreme Court, the cause movements, congressional staff, the nationalized media, and Richard Nixon.

We can argue forever about whether "judge made law" has been good for America or bad. By my lights the Supreme Court's decision in *Brown v. Board of Education* was the affirmative hammer-blow that brought down school segregation. But the Court decisions of the 1970s that interpreted the LBJ civil rights laws as meaning not "Thou Shalt Not Discriminate on the Basis of Race" but "Yes, Thou Shalt," left me cold. *Roe v. Wade* uncovered a new "penumbra" in the Constitution, which turned out to legalize abortion nationally, by a five-to-four vote, at a time when many states had already moved in that direction—New York and California, for example. (Good result, bad legal procedure, as I see it.) The Court's decision came down five years after LBJ left office.

Regardless of your view on substance, few would deny that these were activist courts and that, for a while, they moved the country in a liberal direction. Two points: Most of this happened after the LBJ presidency, and most of it had little to do with the Great Society, a principally legislative achievement.

While many of the "cause movements" (as George McGovern's chief of staff Frank Manckiewicz dubbed them) had roots in the 1960s and even earlier, but they did not erupt in the full flower—or full fury, depending on your point of view—until after President Johnson left office.

It seems elementary, but it is worth remembering that the large majority of Democratic House and Senate members supported President Johnson's Vietnam policy, until his last day in office. The big antiwar demonstrations, with their isolationist overtones, which Johnson condemned, came after his watch. The welfare-rights movement, which encouraged welfare and demanded its extension, came after President Johnson's tenure. The Great Society program included some powerful bedrock environmental laws, but the National Environmental Policy Act didn't pass the Congress until later, and the idea of an "environmental impact statement" was scribbled on the Senate subway by an innocent Scoop Jackson, who expected a two-or-three-page summary of environmental concerns attached to legislation that could affect the environment, and lived to rue the day when the documents were measured by the truckload.

And so it goes. Feminism, gay rights, consumerism, and more, came of age after LBJ. Disruptive? Yes. Good or bad? Perhaps both—your choice. Related to LBJ's Great Society? Hardly.

Over the years the political energy of the cause movements found a home in the rapidly growing number of congressional staffers, the growing power of the independent agencies, and the media. In retrospect, the activist, and leftward, tropism in the media seems to be related to the oft-cited twins "Vietnam and Watergate." I have always found that twinning obscene. Vietnam, for good or for ill, in wisdom or foolishness, was an attempt to help shape the geopolitical destiny of a troubled planet. It may have done that. Watergate was, what? If you believe it was an attempted usurpation of the Constitution, well, I think you're dead wrong. I thought it was a press romp with a president who behaved like a crook, leaving the activist media with an intensified smell of scandal, a tendency that has not redounded to our greater glory in the ensuing years.

Speaking of Richard Nixon, he does play an important part in this tale of misunderstanding of LBJ's Great Society. As more and more history of the time is revealed, it becomes pretty clear that for six years he was the great facilitator of the ideas of the New Left that became commingled in the public mind with the Great Society. The reasons are unclear. Contrary to the notion Nixon cultivated at the time, he was a pretty liberal Republican on many issues. ("Watch what we do, not what we say," said Attorney General John Mitchell early on.) He didn't want to fight on other issues, or he was cowed by the temper of the times. In any event, many of the overextensions of the Great Society occurred on his watch, with his blessing. One example: race preferences in the Labor Department came about with the "Philadelphia Plan," brokered by Under Secretary of Labor Laurence Silberman in the name of the secretary, George Schultz, and the president, Richard Nixon. Its genesis was not the Great Society.

And so it came to pass that President Johnson's Great Society plans came to be linked with the turbulence that followed his term of office.

I remember the late Douglass Cater saying, in his White House office, circa 1967, "It's going to take a little while, but the country will come to appreciate what LBJ has done." There was a recent poll asking respondents who was the best president in the post–World War II period. Johnson finished dead last, at 1 percent, behind Carter, Clinton, and Nixon; John Kennedy was in first place and Ronald Reagan a close second.

OK, so maybe we're not appreciated. Maybe, Doug, it will take a little longer than you thought. LBJ's getting a bum rap. That's too bad. But I know that what LBJ did helped shape America, for the better, and that's what counts.

# The Ship Sails On
## *Joseph A. Califano Jr.*

"Somehow you never forget what poverty and hatred can do when you see its scars on the hopeful face of a young child." With those words President Lyndon Johnson recalled his year as a teacher of poor Mexican children in Cotulla, Texas, as he spoke to a joint session of Congress proposing the Voting Rights Act. It was the evening of March 15, 1965. He continued,

> I never thought then, in 1928, that I would be standing here in 1965. It never even occurred to me in my fondest dreams that I might have the chance to help the sons and daughters of those students and to help people like them all over this country. But now I do have that chance—and I'll let you in on a secret—I mean to use it. And I hope that you will use it with me.

We who shared that opportunity with Lyndon Johnson have vivid recollections of how he drove us to use every second of his presidency: the 5 A.M. calls waking us to ask about a front-page story in the *New York Times* that had not yet been delivered to our homes; the insatiable appetite for a program to cure every ill he saw, or to solve a problem that some Oval Office visitor or wire service story had just brought to his attention; the complaint that we weren't getting Senator Margaret Chase

Smith or a conservative southern House Democrat like Eddie Herbert to vote with us to kill a motion to recommit; the demand for an explanation why the *Washington Post,* or Huntley, Brinkley, or Cronkite, didn't cast their lead stories the way he wanted; the insistence that hearings begin only one day after we sent a bill up to Congress; the pressure to get more seniors enrolled in Medicare, more blacks registered to vote, more schools desegregated, more kids signed up for Head Start, more Mexican-Americans taking college scholarships or loans— and more ugly billboards torn down, faster, for Lady Bird.

His perpetual hunt for simpler, more dramatic ways to explain new programs in shorter sentences led Harry McPherson and me, on one occasion, to write a mock message to Congress, composed completely of three-word sentences; it almost went to Capitol Hill by mistake. Perhaps most disconcerting were the notes from George Christian during a press briefing that conveyed a presidential order to contradict a comment I'd made just a few minutes before; or a presidential command to find some individual out of his past, whose name LBJ could only partially remember, and invite that person to a signing ceremony the next day. Up in heaven, LBJ is probably ordering members of his administration who have passed away to spend more time with deceased senators and representatives to muster support for some celestial program of his. And with every order came Johnson's signature admonition, "Do it now. Not next week. Not tomorrow. Not later this afternoon. Now."

We who served him knew that Lyndon Johnson could be brave and brutal, compassionate and cruel, incredibly intelligent and infuriatingly insensitive. We came to know his shrewd and uncanny instinct for the jugulars of both allies and adversaries. We learned that he could be altruistic and petty, caring and crude, generous and petulant, bluntly honest and calculatingly devious—all within the same few minutes. That his determination to succeed ran over or around whoever and whatever got in his way. That, as allies and enemies around him slumped in exhaustion, his prodigious energy produced second, third, and fourth winds to mount a social revolution and to control everyone and everything around him.

Well, all of that pent-up energy cajoling, driving, and, yes, inspiring each of us to do more than we thought possible did change life in America. In recent years, it is hailed as an accomplishment when a president persuades Congress to pass a few significant bills—even just one, like welfare reform—over an entire congressional session. In today's media world, the voracious quest for television sound bites—or the need to divert attention from scandal—prompts a president routinely to announce initiatives once considered appropriate only for subcabinet officials, mayors, and county commissioners; grants to a few dozen schools or police departments; or release of a new pamphlet issued by the Department of Health and Human Services.

What a contrast. In those tumultuous Great Society years, the president submitted and Congress enacted more than a hundred major proposals in each of the eighty-ninth and ninetieth Congresses! In those years of do-it-now optimism, presidential speeches were about redistributing wealth, overhauling our economic system, reshaping the balance between the consumer and big business, articulating the concept of affirmative action, rebuilding our cities, and eliminating poverty and hunger in our nation.

The complaint heard from Capitol Hill in those years was that the president was promoting too many big ideas at one time.

Well, he was. Why? Because Lyndon Johnson was a revolutionary. He refused to accept pockets of poverty in the richest nation in history. He saw a nation so hell bent on industrial growth and amassing wealth that greed threatened to destroy its natural resources. He saw cities deteriorating and municipal political machines unresponsive to the early migration of Hispanics and the masses of blacks moving north. He saw racial justice as a moral issue, not just a political one. To him government was neither a bad man to be tarred and feathered nor a bagman to collect campaign contributions, but an instrument to help the most vulnerable among us.

The measure of Lyndon Johnson's presidency is how he spent his popularity, not how he accumulated it. For LBJ, popularity—or more properly, his mandate—was something to be disbursed to help the weakest and neediest in our society, not to be husbanded for self-protection. High poll ratings were chips to be shoved into the political pot to pass laws ending segregation and opening voting booths and housing to African Americans and Hispanics.

He had the politician's hunger to be loved. But more than that, he had the courage to fall on his sword if that's what it took to move us closer to a society where "the meaning of our lives matches the marvelous products of our labor." He did just that when, in an extraordinary act of abnegation, he withdrew from the political arena to calm the roiling seas of strife and end the war in Vietnam.

In his view, "The Great Society [asked] not how much, but how good; not only how to create wealth, but how to use it; not only how fast we are going, but where we are headed."

His ambition knew no horizons. He wanted it all. He wanted to be the education president, the health president, the environmental president, the consumer president, the president who eliminated poverty, who gave to the poor the kind of education, health, and social support that most of us get from our parents.

Lyndon Johnson was as much an American revolutionary as George Washington and Thomas Jefferson. Just as their innovations irrevocably reshaped America, his changes set the federal government on a course that it continues to steer to this day despite the conservative, even reactionary, waves that have washed over its bow. Medicare sails on. Student loans and grants sail on. Consumer and environmental protection sails on. His ship—our ship—sails on.

In education, LBJ passed the Elementary and Secondary Education Act, which for the first time committed the federal government to help local school districts. His higher education legislation, with its scholarships, grants, and work-study programs, opened college to any American with the necessary brains and ambition, however thin daddy's wallet or empty mommy's purse. He anticipated the needs of Hispanics with bilingual education, which today serves a million children a year. Special-education legislation bearing his stamp brought help to millions of children with learning disabilities.

Thanks to those Great Society programs, since 1965 the federal government has provided more than 120 billion dollars for elementary and secondary schools; more than a quarter of a trillion dollars in eighty-six million college loans to twenty-nine million students; more than fourteen billion dollars in eighteen million work-study awards to six million students. Today nearly 60 percent of full-time undergraduate students receive federal financial aid under Great Society programs and their progeny. The ship sails on.

What are the fruits for our economy and our society? These programs ensure a steady supply of educated people who enable our industries to lead the world; they provide the human cornerstones for our economic prosperity.

When Lyndon Johnson took office, only 41 percent of Americans had completed high school; only 8 percent held college degrees. By 2000, more than 81 percent had finished high school and 24 percent had completed college. If Johnson's revolution had not established the federal government's responsibility to finance this educational surge, would we have had the trained human resources to be the world's greatest industrial power today? The leading power in computer and information technology? The leading military and communications power? These phenomenal achievements didn't just happen. He moved the fulcrum to offer the opportunity to every American—based on brains, not bucks—to develop his or her talents to the fullest.

And let's not forget Head Start. More than sixteen million preschoolers have been through Head Start programs in just about every city and county in the nation. Today this program serves eight hundred thousand children a year.

How many people remember the battles over Head Start? Conservatives opposed such early-childhood education as an attempt by government to interfere with parental control of their children. In the 1960s those were code words to conjure up images of the Soviet Union wrenching children from their homes to convert them to atheistic communism. But LBJ knew that the rich had kindergartens and nursery schools; why not, he asked, the same benefits for the poor?

And health care. In 1963, most elderly Americans had no health insurance. Few retirement plans provided any such coverage. The poor had little access to medical treatment until they were in critical condition. Only wealthier Americans could get the finest care, and then only by traveling to a few big cities, like Boston or New York.

Is revolution too strong a word? Since 1965, seventy-nine million Americans have signed up for Medicare. In 1966, nineteen million were enrolled; in 1998, thirty-nine million. Since 1966, Medicaid has served more than two hundred million needy Americans. In 1967, it served ten million poor citizens; in 1997, thirty-nine million. The 1968 heart, cancer, and stroke legislation has provided funds to create centers of medical excellence in just about every major city—from Seattle to Houston, Miami to Cleveland, New Orleans to St. Louis and Pittsburgh. To staff these centers, the 1965 Health Professions Educational Assistance Act provided resources to double the number of doctors graduating from medical schools, from eight thousand to sixteen thousand. That act also increased the pool of specialists and researchers, nurses, and paramedics. LBJ's commitment to fund basic medical research lifted the National Institutes of

Health to unprecedented financial heights, seeding a harvest of medical miracles.

Closely related to LBJ's Great Society health programs were his programs to reduce malnutrition and hunger. Today, the Food Stamp program helps feed more than twenty million men, women, and children in more than eight million households. Since it was launched in 1967, the school breakfast program has provided daily breakfasts to nearly a hundred million schoolchildren.

The Great Society has played a pivotal role in the stunning recasting of America's demographic profile. When Johnson took office, life expectancy was 66.6 years for men and 73.1 years for women (69.7 years overall). In a single generation, by 1997, life expectancy jumped 10 percent: for men, to 73.6 years; for women, to 79.2 years (76.5 years overall). The jump was most dramatic among the less advantaged, suggesting that better nutrition and access to health care have played an even larger role than medical miracles. Infant mortality stood at twenty-six deaths for each thousand live births when Johnson took office; today it stands at only 7.3 deaths per thousand live births, a reduction of almost 75 percent. The ship sails on.

It is fair to ask the question, without his programs, would our nation be the world's leader in medical research? In pharmaceutical invention? In creation of surgical procedures and medical machinery to diagnose our diseases, breathe for us, clean our blood, and transplant our organs? Would so much have come about without the basic research fueled by Great Society investments in the National Institutes of Health and in the training of scientific specialists?

Those of us who worked with Lyndon Johnson would hardly characterize him as a patron of the arts. I remember him squirming restlessly, pulling on his ears and rubbing the back of his neck, as he sat at UN Ambassador Arthur Goldberg's Waldorf Towers apartment on the evening before he was scheduled to become the first American president to meet with a pope. Anna Moffo was singing opera—and with each encore I thought Johnson would crawl out of his suit.

Yet one historian—Irving Bernstein, in his book *Guns or Butter: The Presidency of Lyndon Johnson*—titles a chapter, "Lyndon Johnson, Patron of the Arts." Think about it. What would cultural life in America be like without the Kennedy Center for the Performing Arts, the programs of which entertain three million people each year and are televised to millions more; or without the Hirshhorn Museum and Sculpture Garden, which attracts more than seven hundred thousand visitors annually? Both are Great Society accomplishments.

The National Endowments for the Arts and Humanities are fulfilling a dream Johnson expressed when he asked Congress to establish them and have, for the first time, the federal government provide financial support for the arts: "To create conditions under which the arts can flourish; through recognition of achievements, through helping those who seek to enlarge creative understanding, through increasing the access of our people to the works of our artists, and through recognizing the arts as part of the pursuit of American greatness. That is the goal of this legislation."

Johnson used to say that he wanted fine theater and music available throughout the nation and not just on Broadway and at the Metropolitan Opera in New York. In awarding nearly four billion dollars in grants since 1965, the Endowment for the Arts has spawned art councils in all fifty states and more than 420 playhouses, 120 opera companies, four hundred dance companies, and 230 professional orchestras. Since 1965, the Endowment for the Humanities has awarded more than three billion dollars in fifty-six thousand fellowships and grants.

Johnson established the Corporation for Public Broadcasting to create public television and public radio, which have given the nation countless hours of fine arts, superb in-depth news coverage, and educational programs, like *Sesame Street*, that teach as they entertain generations of children. Public television, in fact, invented educational programming for preschool children. Now some say there is no need for public radio and television, with so many cable channels and radio stations. But when you surf with your TV remote or twist your radio dial, you are not likely to find the kind of quality broadcasting that marks the 350 public television and 699 public radio stations that the Corporation for Public Broadcasting supports today. The ship sails on.

Johnson's main contribution to the environment was not the passage of laws but the establishment of a principle that to this day guides the environmental movement. The old principle was simply to conserve resources that had not been touched. Lyndon Johnson was the first president to put forth a larger idea—that we must not only protect the pristine but undertake the additional responsibility of restoring what we had damaged or defiled in the name of development and industrialization. His words in 1965 set the ideological footing for to-day's environmental movement:

> The air we breathe, our water, our soil and wildlife, are being blighted by the poisons and chemicals which are the by-products of technology and industry? The same society which receives the rewards of technol-ogy, as a cooperating whole, take responsibility for control. To deal with these new problems will require a new conservation. We must not only protect the countryside and save it from destruction, we must restore what has been destroyed and salvage the beauty and charm of our cities. Our conservation must be not just the classic conservation of protec-tion and development, but a creative conservation of restoration and innovation.

That new environmental commandment—that we have an obligation to restore as well as preserve, and that those who reap the rewards of mo-dem technology must also pay the price of their industrial pollution—inspired a legion of Great Society laws: the Clear Air, Water Quality and Clean Water Restoration Acts and amendments, the 1965 Solid Waste Disposal Act, the 1965 Motor Vehicle Air Pollution Control Act, the 1968 Aircraft Noise Abatement Act. It also provided the rationale for later laws creating the Environmental Protection Agency and the Super-fund.

Johnson wanted parks close enough for people to enjoy them. Of the thirty-five national parks that he pushed through Congress, thirty-two are within easy driving distance of large cities. The 1968 Wild and Scenic Rivers Act today protects 155 river segments in thirty-seven states. The 1968 National Trail System Act established more than eight hundred recreation, scenic, and historic trails covering forty thousand miles. No wonder *National Geographic* calls Johnson "our greatest conservation pres-ident."

Above all else, Johnson was consumed with creating racial justice and eliminating poverty. Much of the legislation I have mentioned was aimed at those two objectives. But he directly targeted these areas with laserlike intensity.

The social system LBJ faced as he took office featured segregated movie theaters and public accommodations; separate toilets and water fountains for blacks; restaurants and hotels restricted to whites only. Job discrimi-nation was rampant. With the 1964 Civil Rights Act Johnson tore down,

all at once, the "whites only" signs. That law ended segregated public accommodations. No longer would employers be able to discriminate
against blacks. In 1968, one day after the assassination of Martin Luther
King, Johnson sought, characteristically, to find some good even in
tragedy. He pressed House speaker John McCormack to pass the Fair
Housing Act, a bill LBJ had been pushing since 1966. In the wake of that
assassination, Johnson finally got fair housing written into law.

But LBJ knew that laws were not enough. In one of his most moving
speeches, the 1965 Howard University commencement address, entitled,
"To Fulfill These Rights" he said, "But freedom is not enough. You do
not take a person who, for years, has been hobbled by chains and liber-
ate him, bring him to the starting line of a race and then say, 'You are
free to compete with all the others.' And still justly believe that you
have been completely fair. . . . This is the next and the more profound
stage of the battle for civil rights."

Thus was born the concept of affirmative action, Johnson's conviction
that it is essential as a matter of social justice to provide the tutoring, the
extra help, even the preference if necessary, to those who had suffered
generations of discrimination in order to give them a fair chance to share
in the American dream. Perhaps even more controversial today than
when LBJ set it forth, affirmative action has provided opportunity to millions of blacks and has been a critical element of creating a substantial
black middle class, an affluent black society, in a single generation.

That Howard University speech provided another insight that this nation unfortunately ignored. In a catalogue of the long suffering of blacks,
Johnson included this passage:

> Perhaps most important—its influence radiating to every part of life—
> is the breakdown of the Negro family structure. It flows from centuries
> of oppression and persecution of the Negro man. . . . And when the
> family collapses it is the children that are usually damaged. When it
> happens on a massive scale the community itself is crippled. So, unless
> we work to strengthen the family, to create conditions under which
> most parents will stay together—all the rest, schools, and playgrounds,
> and public assistance, and private concern, will never be enough to cut
> completely the circle of despair and deprivation.

If only we had listened to that advice thirty-eight years ago. If only
Congress had heeded his recommendation that welfare benefits no longer

be conditioned on the man leaving the house. What grief we might have saved millions of children and our nation.

In civil rights, indeed in the entire treasury of Great Society measures, the jewel of which the president was proudest—and believed would have the greatest value—was the Voting Rights Act of 1965. That law opened the way for black Americans to strengthen their voices at every level of government. In 1964 there were seventy-nine black elected officials in the South and three hundred in the entire nation. By 1998, there were some nine thousand elected black officials across the nation, including six thousand in the South. In 1965 there were five black members of the House. In 2000 there were thirty-nine.

LBJ's contributions to racial equality were not only civic and political. In 1960, black life expectancy was 63.6 years, not even long enough to benefit from the Social Security taxes that black citizens paid during their working lives. By 1997, black life expectancy was 71.2 years, thanks almost entirely to Medicaid, community health centers, job training, Food Stamps, and other Great Society programs. In 1960, the infant mortality rate for blacks was 44.3 for each thousand live births; in 1997, that rate had plummeted by two-thirds, to 14.7. In 1960, only 20 percent of blacks completed high school and only 3 percent college; in 1997, 75 percent completed high school and more than 13 percent earned college degrees. The ship sails on.

Most of the laws I have noted were part of LBJ's War on Poverty. He used every tool at his disposal to wage this war, the war on which he had set his heart. Though he found the opposition too strong to pass an income-maintenance law, he took advantage of the biggest automatic cash machine available—Social Security. He proposed, and Congress enacted, whopping increases in the minimum benefits that lifted 2.5 million Americans sixty-five and over above the poverty line, in "the greatest stride forward since Social Security was launched in 1935." In 1996, Social Security lifted twelve million senior citizens above the poverty line. The ship sails on.

The combination of that Social Security increase, Medicare, and the coverage of nursing home care under Medicaid (which funds care for 68 percent of nursing home residents) has had a defining impact on American families. Millions of middle-aged Americans, freed from the burden of providing medical and nursing home care for their elderly parents, suddenly were able to buy homes and (often with an assist from Great Society higher education programs) send their children to college. This salutary and pervasive impact has led many scholars to cite Medicare and Social Security as the most significant social programs of the twentieth century.

Johnson's relationship with his pet project—the Office of Economic Opportunity—was that of a proud father often irritated by an obstreperous child. For years conservatives have raged about the OEO programs. Yet Johnson's War on Poverty was founded on the most conservative of principles—put the power in the local community, not in Washington; give people at the grassroots the ability to stand on their own two feet, and to stand tall, off the federal welfare dole.

Conservative claims to have killed the OEO poverty programs are preposterous—as fanciful as Ronald Reagan's quip that Lyndon Johnson declared war on poverty and poverty won. As of the year 2000, eleven of the twelve programs that OEO launched are alive, well, and funded at an annual rate exceeding ten billion dollars. They have grown by almost 1,000 percent since their inception in 1965. Head Start, Job Corps, Community Health Centers, Foster Grandparents, Upward Bound (now part of the Trio Program in the Department of Education), Green Thumb (now Senior Community Service Employment), Indian Opportunities (now in the Labor Department), and Migrant Opportunities (now Seasonal Worker Training and Migrant Education) were all designed to do what they have been doing—empowering individuals to stand tall on their own two feet.

Community Action, VISTA Volunteers, and Legal Services were designed to put power in the hands of individuals—down at the grassroots. The grassroots that these programs fertilize don't produce just the manicured laws that conservatives prefer. Of all the Great Society programs started in the Office of Economic Opportunity, only the Neighborhood Youth Corps has been abandoned—in 1974, after enrolling more than five million individuals. Despite the political rhetoric, every president has urged Congress to fund these OEO programs or approved substantial appropriations for them. The ship sails on.

When LBJ took office, 22.2 percent of Americans were living in poverty. When he left, only 13 percent were living below the poverty line. By the year 2000, the poverty level stood at 13.3 percent, still disgraceful in the context of what was the greatest economic boom in our history. But what if the Great Society had not achieved that dramatic reduction in poverty? What if the nation had not maintained that reduction? There would today be twenty-four million more Americans living below the poverty level.

Johnson confronted two monumental shifts in America: the urbanization of the population and the nationalization of commercial power.

For urban America, he drove through Congress the Urban Mass Transit Act. Among other things, that law gave San Franciscans BART, Washingtonians the Metro, Atlantans MARTA, and cities across America thousands of buses and modernized transit systems. His 1968 Housing Act has provided housing for more than seven million families. He created Ginnie Mae, which has added more than a trillion dollars to the supply of affordable mortgage funds. He privatized Fannie Mae, which has helped more than thirty million families purchase homes. He established the Department of Housing and Urban Development, naming the first black cabinet member to be its secretary. And he put financial muscle in the National Trust for Historic Preservation to preserve historic, including urban, treasures.

Johnson also faced the rise of the national grocery and retail chains and enormous corporate enterprises—a nationalization of commercial power that had the potential to disadvantage the individual American consumer. As he took office, superstores and super-corporations were rapidly shoving aside the corner grocer, local banker, and independent drug store. Automobiles were complex and dangerous, manufactured by giant corporations with deep pockets to protect themselves. Banks had the most sophisticated accountants and lawyers to draft their loan agreements. Sellers of everyday products—soaps, produce, meats, appliances, clothing, cereals, and canned and frozen foods—packaged their products with the help of the shrewdest marketers and designers. The individual was outflanked at every position.

Sensing that mismatch, Johnson pushed through Congress a bevy of laws to level the playing field for consumers: auto and highway safety legislation for the car buyer and motorist; truth in packaging for the housewife; truth in lending for the home buyer, small businessman, and individual borrower; meat and wholesome poultry laws to enhance food safety. He created the Product Safety Commission to ensure that toys and other products would be safe for users; he had passed the Flammable Fabrics Act to reduce the incendiary characteristics of clothing and blankets. To keep kids out of the medicine bottle he proposed the Child Safety Act.

The revolution in transportation and its importance to the nation led to Johnson's decision to ram through Congress the Department of Transportation and the National Transportation Safety Board, combining more than thirty independent agencies to help rationalize the nation's transportation system.

By the numbers, the legacy of Lyndon Johnson is monumental. It exceeds in domestic impact even the New Deal of his idol, Franklin Roosevelt. But I believe that LBJ's legacy is far more profound and lasting. He recognized that laws and programs were written not in stone but on a blackboard of history that can be changed or erased. LBJ's most enduring legacy is not in the numbers and the statistics of programs but in the fundamental tenets of public responsibility that he espoused. Those tenets influence and shape the nation's public policy and political dialogue to this day.

Until the New Deal, the federal government had been regarded as a regulatory power, protecting the public health and safety with the Food and Drug Administration, and enforcing antitrust and commercial fraud laws to rein in concentrations of economic power. With the creation of the Securities and Exchange and Interstate Commerce Commissions and the other "alphabet" agencies, FDR took the government into deeper regulatory waters. He also put the feds into the business of cash handouts to the needy: welfare payments, railroad retirement, and Social Security.

Johnson converted the federal government into a far more energetic, proactive force for social justice—striking down discriminatory practices, offering a hand up with education, health care, and job training. These functions had formerly been the preserves of private charities and the states. Before the Johnson administration, for example, the federal government was not training a single worker. He vested the federal government with responsibility to soften the sharp elbows of capitalism and give it a human, beating heart; to redistribute opportunity as well as wealth. In education, Johnson postulated a new right—the right of all individuals to all the education they needed to develop their talents, regardless of their economic circumstances.

He had a penetrating prescience. He saw the frightful implications of savaging "the Negro family"; He called "the welfare system in America outmoded and in need of a major change" and pressed Congress to create "a work incentive program, incentives for earning, day care for children, child and maternal health and family planning services."

He saw the threat posed by the spread of guns and proposed, in 1968, national registration of all guns and national licensing of all gun owners.

Congress rejected his proposals. But he did convince Capitol Hill to close the loophole of mail-order guns, prohibit sales to minors, and end the import of "Saturday-night specials."

He spotted the "for sale" signs of political corruption going up in the nation's capital. Accordingly, he proposed public financing of presidential campaigns, full disclosure of contributions and expenses by all federal candidates, limits on the amount of contributions, and closure of lobbying loopholes. In 1967, he warned of the problems that plague our political life today:

> More and more, men and women of limited means may refrain from running for public office. Private wealth increasingly becomes an artificial and unrealistic arbiter of qualifications, and the source of public leadership is thus severely narrowed. The necessity of acquiring substantial funds to finance campaigns diverts a candidate's attention from his public obligations and detracts from his energetic exposition of the issues.

To me, Johnson's greatest quality was one not often mentioned as an LBJ trait—his courage. His means were often Machiavellian, but he was a true believer. He believed, and he fought for what he believed in, no matter how it hurt him politically. He fought for racial equality even when it hurt him and clobbered his party in the South. He fought to end poverty, even when it hurt him and subjected him to ridicule. And yes, he fought the war in Vietnam—and that hurt.

He was willing to fall upon his sword for what he thought was right. He viewed his soaring popularity, in the wake of his landslide against Barry Goldwater, not as something to be hoarded but as something to be poured out on behalf of those who didn't have shoes to pound the pavements of power. Lyndon Johnson didn't talk the talk of legacy; he walked the walk. He lived the life. He didn't have much of a profile—but he did have courage.

Why then does current history, along with Democratic politicians, so ignore him? Why did Bill Clinton, presidential candidate, come to the LBJ Library during the 1992 campaign and never speak the name of Lyndon Johnson? Why do Democratic House and Senate leaders rarely invoke his name even as they battle to preserve and build on his legacy?

The answers lie in their fear of being called "liberal," and in the Vietnam War.

In contemporary America, politicians want to be called anything but liberal; they are paralyzed by fear of the liberal label that comes with the heritage of Lyndon Johnson. Democrats rest their hopes on promises to preserve and expand Great Society programs like Medicare and aid to education, but they tremble at the thought of linking those programs to the liberal Lyndon. The irony is that they seek to distance themselves from the president who once said that the difference between liberals and cannibals is that cannibals eat only their enemies.

Democratic officeholders also assign Johnson the role of "stealth president," because of the Vietnam War. Most contemporary observers put the war down as a monumental blunder. Only a handful—most of them Republicans—defend Vietnam as part of a half-century bipartisan commitment to contain communism with American blood and money. Seen in that context, Vietnam was a tragic losing battle in a long, winning war—a war that began with Truman's ordeal in Korea, the Marshall Plan, and the 1948 Berlin airlift, and ended with the collapse of communism at the end of the Reagan administration.

Let everyone think what they will about Vietnam—and let the politicians shrink from the liberal label. But let us all recognize the reality of this revolutionary's remarkable achievements. When Lyndon Johnson surveyed history, he observed that World War II had killed Roosevelt's New Deal and that the Korean War killed Harry Truman's Fair Deal. The Vietnam War slowed Johnson's domestic crusade—but it did not kill it.

Indeed, the tension that marked Johnson's presidency arose from his refusal to let Vietnam destroy his Great Society. His concentration on domestic progress amid the incredible sound and fury of those years was phenomenal. His determination was fierce, and it was articulated most powerfully in his 1966 State of the Union message:

> We will continue to meet the needs of our people by continuing to develop the Great Society. . . . There are men who cry out: We must sacrifice. Well, let us rather ask them: Who will they sacrifice? Are they going to sacrifice the children who seek the learning, or the sick who need medical care, or the families who dwell in squalor now brightened by the hope of a home? Will they sacrifice opportunity for the distressed, the beauty of our land, the hope of our poor? . . . I believe that we can continue the Great Society while we fight in Vietnam. But if there are some who do not believe this, then, in the name of justice, let them call for the contribution of those who live in the fullness of our

blessing, rather than try to strip it from the hands of those that are most in need.

Johnson's critics derided this as a profligate call for "guns and butter." But it was vintage LBJ—and it too reflected his unquenchable courage and determination.

The sharpest attacks on LBJ's Vietnam policies came from George Mc-Govern, the South Dakota senator and antiwar Democratic presidential candidate in 1972. In 1999, McGovern placed Johnson alongside Woodrow Wilson and Franklin Roosevelt as one of the greatest presidents since Abraham Lincoln. "Johnson did more than any other president to advance civil rights, education, and housing, to name just three of his concerns," McGovern wrote. Citing Johnson's opposition, when he was majority leader, to any U.S. involvement in Vietnam, McGovern concluded; "If it had been up to Lyndon Johnson we would have not gone to Vietnam in the first place. It would be a historic tragedy if his outstanding domestic record remained forever obscured by his involvement in a war he did not begin and did not know how to stop."

As the century ended, another critic of LBJ on the Vietnam War, John Kenneth Galbraith—Harvard University economist, ambassador to India, and liberal activist—placed Lyndon Johnson "next only to Franklin D. Roosevelt as a force for a civilized and civilizing social policy essential for human well-being and for peaceful co-existence between the economically favored (or financially fortunate) and the poor. . . . Next only to Roosevelt, and in some respects more so, Lyndon Johnson was the most effective advocate of humane social change in the United States in this century."

At his best, Lyndon Johnson put the thumb of government forcefully on the scale for the vulnerable among us. He hauled and dragooned talented people into public service, a calling he considered the highest an individual could have. At the risk of nagging, he reminded the American people that God and history would judge us not just on how much our gross national product grew but on how we spent it; not simply on how many millionaires a booming economy produced but on how many millions of people it lifted out of poverty.

In the last speech of his life, when his civil rights papers were opened to the public, Lyndon Johnson had this to say: "Well, this cry of 'Never' I've heard since I was a little boy, all my life. And what we commemorate this great day is some of the work which has helped to make 'never' now."

Through it all—the war, the hurt, the sometimes devious and crude behavior, the haunting ghosts of the Kennedys, the ambition for his country and himself, during what LBJ called "the most serious" times "confronted by the nation in the course of my lifetime"—he never lost his concentration on trying "to make 'never' now." He left us plenty of achievements to build on— achievements that in my judgment far outweigh the mistakes he left us.

It is time now for his heirs to recognize—and, yes, for history to recognize—that no president ever cared more, tried harder, or helped more needy Americans.

The waves of his critics may crash against the bow of his efforts and his record. But the record is there. The ship—his ship, our ship—sails on.

# About the Contributors

**Hyman Bookbinder** was formerly the Top Office of Economic Opportunity Aide to Sargent Shriver, an American Jewish Committee Leader, chair of Public Policy Advocates for Public Broadcasting (1972–1977), and founding member of the National Jewish Democratic Council. He has authored a number of books with James C. Abourzok, including *Through Different Eyes: Two Leading Americans, a Jew and an Arab Debate U.S. Policy in the Middle East.*

**Joseph A. Califano Jr.** was special assistant for Domestic Affairs under Johnson and former Secretary of Health, Education, and Welfare (1977–1979). Currently he is the chairman and president of the Center on Addiction and Substance Abuse at Columbia University, an independent nonprofit research center affiliated with Columbia University, an adjunct professor of public health at Columbia University's Medical School and School of Public Health, and a member of the Institute of Medicine of the National Academy of Sciences. He is an expert in health care delivery and cost-containment, and has lectured extensively about America's health care system. He is the author of nine books and has written numerous articles for prominent newspapers and leading journals.

**Thomas W. Cowger** is professor of history at East Central University, Ada, Oklahoma. He is the author of *The National Congress of American Indians: The Founding Years* and several articles in academic journals. He has been awarded numerous fellowships, grants, and teaching awards.

**James Cross** was a brigadier general in the U.S. Air Force, the Pilot of Air Force One, and a military aide to President Johnson. He performed a tour of duty in Vietnam, was commander of the 75th Tactical Reconnaissance Wing at Bergstrom Air Force Wing. His military decorations include the Legion of Merit, Distinguished Flying Cross, Air Medal, Air Force Outstanding Unit Award Ribbon with oak leaf cluster, and Presidential Service Badge. He is now retired.

**Ervin S. Duggan** was staff assistant in the Johnson White House, deputy to the late Douglass Cater, and President Johnson's chief aide on education matters. He was also president and CEO of PBS, former commissioner of the Federal Communications Commission, and helped to craft the Public Broadcasting Act. He has held numerous public service posts, including special assistant to Senators Lloyd Bentsen and Adlai Stevenson III, special assistant to HEW Secretary Joseph Califano; and was a member of the U.S. State Department's policy planning staff under Secretaries Cyrus Vance and Edmund Muskie. He has coauthored with Ben J. Wattenberg *Against All Enemies*. He has also written numerous articles in leading journals.

**Luci Baines Johnson** is President Lyndon Baines Johnson's daughter; chairman of the board of the LBJ Holding Company, vice president of the BusinesSuites, and a member of the board of directors of LBJ Broadcasting. She serves in a number of professional and public capacities and has long served on countless board of directors, advisory councils, and as a trustee for various organizations and other leadership positions. She has received numerous honors and awards including the 1997 Top 25 Women-Owned Businesses by the *Austin Business Journal* and K-EYE TV, the Distinguished Service Award from Georgetown University School of Nursing, the Apollo Award, the "Special Friend" Award from the University of Texas, Austin, and honorary membership in Sigma Theta Tau. She established the Luci Baines Johnson Centennial Professorship in Nursing at the University of Texas, Austin.

**Nicholas deBelleville Katzenbach** was former U.S. Attorney General (1965–1966), Under Secretary of State (1966–1969), senior vice president and general counsel of IBM. He published with Morton A. Kaplan *The Political Foundations of International Law* as well as many articles for professional journals.

**Lawrence Levinson** was chief assistant to Joseph Califano, executive president and member of the Board of Paramount Communications (1967–1994), partner of Verner Liipfert, Bernard, McPherson & Hand (1994–present), Washington, D.C.

**Sherwin J. Markman** was congressional relations staff, later assistant to President Johnson, and a retired senior partner for Hogan & Hartson, Washington, D.C., where he represented some noted clients and was involved in several important cases. He published a best selling novel, *The Election*, which was translated into Russian by the former U.S.S.R. Following retirement, he spent eight years as a long distance sailor. He has recently contracted with St. Martin's Press to write a biography on President Johnson from the perspective of Chief of Staff W. Marvin Watson.

**Jack McNulty** was speechwriter and later assistant to President Johnson, speechwriter for a succession of General Motors chairmen, and vice-president over GM's public relations staff. After retirement, he has owned a horse stable and raced thoroughbreds in Kentucky and elsewhere.

**Harry Middleton** was a speechwriter for President Johnson, helped the president prepare his memoirs, and former longtime director of the LBJ Library and Museum in Austin, Texas. He also authored *LBJ: The White House Years*.

**Peter R. Rosenblatt** was deputy assistant general counsel for the Near East and South Asia region, USAID, Department of State (1966), on the White House National Security Staff (1966–1968), and judicial officer and chairman for Board of Contract Appeals, U.S. Post Office Department (1968–1969). He was also ambassador and President Carter's personal representative to the negotiations on the Future Political Status of Trust Territory of the Pacific Islands (1977–1981). He has practiced law and been involved in several business interests, including recently serving as a founder and president of Fund for Democracy and Development. He also continues to serve as adviser on foreign policy.

**Jack Valenti** was special assistant to President Johnson, president and CEO of the Motion Picture Association of America. He has written four books: *The Bitter Taste of Glory, A Very Human President, Speak Up with Confidence,* and *Protect and Defend.* He has written numerous essays for leading newspapers, popular journals, and magazines. France awarded him its highly prized the French Legion of Honor. He has been awarded his own star on Hollywood's Walk of Fame. He has been named a lifetime member of the Directors Guild of America.

**Ben Wattenberg** was a speechwriter for President Johnson and a senior fellow at American Institute in Washington, D.C. He writes a weekly syndicated column and has been the host of several public affairs television series. He is a former contributing editor of *U.S. News and World Report* and is author or coauthor of numerous books, including, *Values Matter Most: How Republicans or Democrats or a Third Party Can Win, and Renew the American Way of Life.*

**Lee White** was special counsel to Presidents Kennedy and Johnson, chairman of the Federal Power Commission, and a partner with Semer, White and Jacobsen in Washington, D.C.